PRAISE FOR MASCULINITY AMIDST MADNESS

"Ryan Landry does the yeoman work of addressing how we should collectively go about repairing one damaged foundation of society: masculinity. Masculinity is the source from which security and order spring forth into the world, and consequently, the gynocratic attack upon masculinity during late modernity has crippled the security and order of our society. In *Masculinity Among Madness,* he examines what masculinity is, why it matters, the ways in which masculinity has been corrupted in late modernity, and then providing an action plan by which each individual can reclaim and revitalize their masculinity." — Micah Jenkins

"The perfect companion piece to *Bronze Age Mindset:* whereas BAP used a rousing form and esoteric mysticism to excite the remnants of the masculine spirit lying dormant in the reader, toxified by modern culture, Landry identifies the components of our toxic culture, analyzing them in detail, and provides a practical, actionable battle plan to fight the vultures insistent upon men being reduced to consumer weaklings, ashamed of themselves and their heritage. *Masculinity Among Madness* is the next step in reclaiming the masculine soul and forging a future we were meant to inherit!" — "Bad" Billy Pratt, *Kill to Party*

"Masculinity is in deep crisis. Most men simply don't know what it means to be a man who can protect and provide for their families. Author Ryan Landry fully understands this modern problem and has written a book that begins to repair the damage that society has wrought upon men. He eloquently explains the crisis and offers practical solutions to reignite the birthright of the Western man. Hopefully, his book will be read by the generation of young men today to block out efforts of the culture to feminize and weaken them." — Roosh Valizadeh, author of *Lady*

MASCULINITY AMIDST MADNESS

RYAN LANDRY

Sheridan, WY
Terror House Press
2020

ISBN 978-1-951897-14-7

EDITOR

Matt Forney (mattforney.com)

FRONT COVER DESIGN

Owen Cyclops (owencyclops.com)

LAYOUT AND BACK COVER DESIGN

Matt Lawrence (mattlawrence.net)

TERROR HOUSE PRESS, LLC

terrorhousepress.com

TABLE OF CONTENTS

"Do not believe those who say life goes fast. Life is a slow march for our souls in this world. These are truths for a soul who recognizes this fact and wishes to triumph. Old truths shall be spoken. Words passed on from generation to generation grace these pages. Some have forgotten them. Some never learned them. Some run from them. Read them, speak them, and share them, so that none forget." — Ryan Landry

FOREWORD
by Bronze Age Pervert

My friend wrote this book to help you stop being the catamite you are and help you become the man nature will allow you to be. He speaks of war! This how the book begins to teach you to be a man, because original title of Man was reserved for warrior only. The rest were persons, vague individuals. Not real men. Stop being an "individual" and become a man! An individual is just "some guy." Nobody cares about modern "lifestyle choices": it's consumer accessories, it's prefab faggotry! Caesar felt like a faggot when he compared himself to Alexander. This spurred him to great heights. You're so much faggot you can't even imagine what it's like to compare yourself to Alexander and feel the spur to great action.

Great action! But don't confuse this with little action. This is not a book about ambition. Remember the man of power Bob Denard. He was a merc and adventurer who took over the Comoros Islands several times in the 20th Century. France had to send special forces to dislodge him, or he surely would have become worshipped as a god by the natives. Yet he was never ambitious, never a kissass. In his youth, he got kicked out of the French military for burning a bar in Vietnam, and then was a hooligan in Africa. He became a man of power and international mercenary. The paradox: if you don't feel like a faggot compared to Denard, you are, in fact, a faggot.

Denard said the ambitious are pretenders and worthless: a real man does what he must and is driven by great and single-minded passion. He isn't driven by "status." The ambitious today are regime loyalists. They are the type of males who work 80 hours a week to become interior designer or push homopedosubmission from the corrupt political class. Status is fake, honor is real. This book teaches the way of honor. Honor appears among strong animal, too: all real men have respected animal of power like bear, lion, eagle. Man has too much monkey in him, maybe. But also, there is something else in us, from somewhere else, to deny the inner monkey. To seek honor, which is in nature. Tranny freaks in our time have great "status," but Denard is a man of great action who lived by drive for honor. Patton, too. Many such cases. This book begins to open the path!

Great action is hard today. Our enemy doesn't fight in the open, but scurries under sewers and tries to poison with the fumes of rot under these cities. These aren't cities we live in, but steaming Oriental rabbit-piles of scurrying humanity, built on Calcutta-style garbage landfills. My friend teaches you to shrug that off; their straitjacket is on your mind only. It holds no power if you steel yourself with the right practices and right mind. They use sometimes mycotoxins and estrogens too, though, to attack the nervous system: he teaches how to fight that as well with various exercises, with friendship, with foods!

Friendship is our path out of this modern disaster. Brotherhoods and friendships of strong, brave men will be able to change our condition. Make yourself strong and worthy of a good friend. This book has wise words about friendship, real friendship.

This book I believe was written under compulsion of a shadow—I have seen it too—under berry bushes full of thorns just before midnight in a forest…I fear to speak of it…it was so dark, under neon shades of ultramarine blue beside old buildings of corrugated steel. Every time I've walked through it past midnight, strange orchids bloomed around every step I took! This shadow whispered in my ear, it said, "I ward off the dwarf of the sixth hour." The fragrance of flowers and musty fruit in the forest at night is all I remember. He talks of this forest in this book, alludes to it, but you have to see if you find the path back through time. If you don't read this book and take his advice, I fear you will surely remain a pathic and fall into the bottomless swamps of Hades.

Ancient men despised Hades. They thought this zombie kingdom of Hades was full of refuse and terror. Why? Because it was dirty, turgid, boring, lifeless, and bloodless. That is true terror. Think of a nightmare where you open a door only to end up in the same room over and over.

This is what Hades was. And we are in Hades, or they're trying to force us there—be sure about that! Just indistinct, boring existence until the end of time. 40,000 years of the 56 percent. The myths of Sisyphus and Tantalus were hell for the Greeks: endless meaningless repetition of labor to no end, brute desire that isn't ever satisfied. Without the grace of high spirit and manly mission, you risk falling into this pit very soon. You are probably there now! Most of the world is. THEY ARE DOOMED!

What is the path out? There are many ways to take, and many are hinted at in this book. This book teaches the path of strength. Many of you have liked my saying:

> *"Ancient men conquered cities put them to the sword and fire, meanwhile you go to WINE BAR with 'gf' and enjoy tasteful banter... YOU ARE GAY!"*

Some attaqd me for this. They said ancient men were also men of taste and refinement, attended wine party, attended feast, knew how to be gentle with women. They said look at *The Book of the Courtier,* look at samurai who had to have some training in the arts, appreciation of aesthetics. Yes, but it's easier to refine and cultivate a rough man who's a barbarian than to teach an exhausted manikin to be a man. Gentleness and easy living is too frequent in our age; true manliness is rare. Pursue manliness and be uncompromisingly brave, because at least it's rare. It's not good to be too spread out in too many directions. A man must be one-minded and have purity of purpose. This is what's lacking in our time; this is what is rare.

Greeks worshiped Achilles. He chose death! He could have chosen a long and comfortable life. Greeks had a word for this kind of life: "by his mother's side." It was almost poetic formula. It's said of Jason, leader of the Argonauts and his crew, and of what they chose against. But Jason and his crew chose instead a great voyage into the unknown and great fame. Achilles chose a short life of war, and he chose death to avenge his friend. He thereby won eternal fame among men. Theseus chose danger, a great voyage, the Labyrinth: he saved his homeland from a foreign beast that devoured its choicest young every year. Who will be our Theseus?

This is an old formula. It exists in many Indo-European languages. I am told it was the song of a beautiful goddess, purple-magenta skin and lime-green eyes, who haunted the deep tropical forests around the North Pole circa 10,000 BC. I've seen those forests! There was emerald and sapphire growing on baobabs like fruit, and you could eat them. Watch Bach's *St. Matthew Passion* and you will see Jesus shown in this same heroic way: a supreme being of great courage who stands out from the herd of subhumans.

Who knows how Trump will turn out? But in our time, Trump has been treated the same as Jesus was by the Philistine crony establishment, by Babylon. He shows the path forward because he was the only brave man in our time, and chose the path of danger and great fame, not material comfort. The thing that is most lacking now is bravery and courage. Remember that, seek it, and steel yourself for the future. The Greek word for courage was "manliness!"

Remember the saying of Heraclitus: "the best choose one thing above others, eternal glory among mortals: but the many glut themselves like livestock." To become a real man is a spiritual path. The path to eternity begins with manliness. This path lies hidden, but there are many keys, many doors. This book, a fatherly exhortation, begins to teach you the way of power.

Bronze Age Pervert

2017

MASCULINITY AMIDST MADNESS

CHAPTER 1

There is a war all around you. It is not a silent war, but in your face from all angles. The enemy deploys columns and weapons where you work and where your children go to school. Its propaganda, overt and covert, subverts your mind through every form of media. This is the spiritual war against men.

Masculine virtues are attacked. The natural order of life is upended, and this upending is not for the benefit of women, but rather the elites who want dependent, weak people. These weak people themselves, not realizing how they got this way, want still more restraints on the masculine. They want men and women with feminine values. The elites and their coalitions of the weak would have us all adopt a peasant worldview wherein we cede all sovereignty to the central authority.

To read this means you do not laugh off such an idea. You realize that men may roll their eyes at this declaration and pretend to be above it all, but the other side is always plotting new ways to attack, destroy, and demoralize. They want you to give up and ease into the sleepy security of consumer hedonism. They want you enslaved and too distracted, tired, and weak to object.

Do not sleepwalk through this life. The world responds to one's actions. The spark, the mood that hits to get out, walk, fight, do something. This is the spark that drives life. How does one go through this life? Speak and live as the man people will not just want to meet, but to follow. Mold yourself into the iron that no magnets can resist. This is the age of Peter Pan, the man-child, and nominal adults. The person one presents should be the man of order among the chaos and children. We are not women or children, but men.

Do not blame your father. Do not blame your mother. This is your life. The choice to understand the man you are and are capable of becoming is yours. Each man is capable of beautiful acts of light and monstrous deeds of darkness. We must seek the light and remember the dangerous nature residing in us all. Having standards, living up to them, and enforcing them does not make you an evil man. Acts of kindness and virtue are found even in the simplest no.

The easier path, the path of least resistance, is a coward's way to travel through life. What is man's journey but a struggle against the physical and spiritual obstacles of this world? You will need to study and train. You will need to govern and harness your emotions. And you will need to be judicious with your speech and in the selection of your friends. Do not deny the need to see the problems at hand, the problems at large, and the problems of the future. Develop your mind and body, find other good men, and have the courage to lead when you can. Develop your will, drive, and the ability to follow through. Do not complain like a child or a peasant, but act like the men who came before you, who struck out to conquer and build.

Ours is a time of shying from challenges, of timid men cowed with the fear of failure. Remember that we can only develop our faculties through our earnest efforts and failures. You may have seen this burning out or turtling in an older man, perhaps a father, uncle, or friend, one who in youth was a man of spirit, who had energy and confidence. Something happened, though. The wild exploits ended, the stories became more and more immediate, and his life became insular and safe. In the worst of cases, you can say that some of these men die but that we only bury their bodies 50 years later.

It is not simply age, because you can see this in men in their twenties. The banter they had with friends and family is subdued now. Forget the roaring laughter they had filled a room with; you can't even get them angry. But we all know an older man who still wields a sharp tongue, still has passion for his pursuits, and still laughs with gusto. Nor is it domestication. There are plenty of men with wives and children that will still introduce you to a new drink, tell you about an author they have discovered, or show you the motorcycle they are restoring. When a man's fire has gone out, it is because he did not tend it. He let the world smother it.

The Greeks would say that these men lacked *thumos.* The passion and spirit that coursed through their blood evaporated. It is not entirely their fault, as these men were not even told of this spiritual fire. No one explained how it resides in all men. Ancient man looked to the night sky and saw his gods. Our grandfathers looked up and saw worlds to reach. Modern men deny the stars their respect and look at their phones. Challenges seem too risky. They forget what they are capable of doing. They become dulled by the messages of society, rather than listening to their drives and the voices of history.

The walk in the forest at night is a challenge and full of danger. At first, it is so dark your eyes may as well be closed, but in a few minutes, they adjust. You see forms, shapes. Vision slowly improves. Venture into the forest each night and your anxiety wanes as the noises become familiar. You begin to identify smells and can sense when it has rained or the forest is beginning a seasonal change. Autumn has a distinct smell just as spring does. In time, a night walk through the forest becomes an easy stroll.

We navigate such realms daily. Media bombards the senses and floods the mind with never-ending new information. Seek the truth, the time tested. Eliminate the silly and useless thoughts poured into your mind by others. In any journey, during any task, there will be detractors. Unless they are walking with you and working with you, they are not worth any thought.

That which can be done today should be done immediately. The future is full of unknown tasks that may prevent you from accomplishing today's challenge. Do not flow with the masses. You are descended from a man who set off into the unknown to build a life. His blood is your blood. Do not succumb to the superficial fads marketed to you by faceless others. A life filled with hollow pursuits becomes hollow itself. The lust for power, the lust for strength are always within you. Our society smothers you with comforts and dulls the senses with hedonism.

When you forget the eternal and succumb to the immediate, the system's information flow distracts you from sorting out yourself and your immediate circle. Some are gifted with strong wills, and others must develop this skill, but willpower is available to us all. Start with daily denials and rituals, and as healthy habits become instinctive, you will feel your power grow.

Do not completely avoid those who don't choose this path, but try to help them, and if they don't respond, glean lessons from their lives. Learn to notice and correct little changes in yourself when you happen to stray from your path. Develop strength, physically, intellectually, and emotionally. Learn when to reveal that strength. Like Faust, there should be a hunger for always a little more from your life, for new challenges.

Before entering any argument, consider the opponent, the issue, and the potential gain. The zealot will not be converted, or the situation may offer no gain. But to withdraw into a peaceful secluded life is no victory for the soul. Nothing worth having is earned easily or given, contentment included.

Do not view friends for what they can do for you. Friendship is not an accounting sheet with credits and debits. Do not give into the transactional nature of contemporary friendship. In times of chaos, the man who can find and tell the truth in a confident manner will win friends. Even mere acquaintances will seek your judgment and guidance in times of need. Don't let youth be an excuse. The young man who can resist the temptations of mass society will impress and inspire those of any age. Your path may be difficult, but face it with clear eyes and faith in yourself to accomplish. Do not settle for easy tasks and do not stop challenging yourself. Contemporary man is a slave to status for any ever-changing definition of what is good, like the man chasing the piper and not marching with the tune. Set yourself to time-tested standards and the petty whispers will go silent as the melody of righteousness guides you.

Be careful of the man who speaks of equality. The further from himself the grievance he wishes to address, the more likely he is hiding mistreatment of those closest to him. Can you not see him and observe the inequalities between you two?

Develop your character and mastery of your emotions so that you can better present yourself. Many contemporary men, feeling powerless, are offended easily and use hyperbole to express offense. Learn to respond appropriately to nuisances. A child's control of emotions will beget a child's control of speech. A man knows he must master his emotions, his words, and himself before he can be a leader or judge of other men. This judgment is critical, as a man must know his limitations.

A man knows that to learn means more than to simply ask questions. It means more than reading one book. It means more than a simple search on a phone. A man knows to question the veracity of claims and to seek pure truth. Armed not just with the truth, but with a drive and method for discovering the truth, a man can trust his judgment. If a man can trust his judgment, he can trust himself to be a fair judge of other men. From there, he can lead.

A common refrain from the man who leaves schooling whether at eighteen or in his twenties is "how am I doing?" It hits at weddings or hearing a friend is expecting a kid. There are life events that one uses as a measure. Those can be misleading. No one knows the full story or circumstances behind these life events so using them as a measurement is a poor choice. The introspection inspired by the event is positive. They still point to a need that our society has pushed away: goals.

Focus goals on your capabilities, not material wealth. You live in a consumer society geared to create an ever-present need to consume and accumulate more. Gauging yourself by the possessions of others will never leave you satisfied. There is always something new to buy. Our culture comes with designated advertising breaks to make sure to poke at you that you need more stuff. At its core, advertising is telling you to be unsatisfied with everything except the very thing they are selling you. Material wealth can be taken away at any moment. A rich man and a useful man can both be made bankrupt, but who will be drafted first in a moment of crisis when all the money is gone? The useful man.

These goals are about you as a man in this world. The object of goals is to build and refine your skills to hit them, earning the achievement. The goals you set must be reachable but challenge your present ability. Whether through a daily grind or sudden breakthrough, hitting your goal must come with knowledge that a struggle occurred.

A society focused on liberating the individual will destroy the need for goals because they are arbitrary measures or forced on person by a judgmental society. This supposedly hinders true development or straightjackets the enlightened, fabulous individual within as a man is forced to comply with norms or mores. What this does is leave the individual roaming adulthood with no markers except discovering something new. This idea of discovery becomes a process, eventually becoming a habit where more extreme experiences are sought just for the vital feeling of new. This itself is a goal imposed by an outside force, but the outside force is our current cultural tastemakers.

Goals are needed. We must know if we have failed or succeeded. To live life just drifting through is to become enveloped with fog. To meet a goal, no matter how small, is a win. Life is full of wins outside how we individually perform, so our personal behavior and efforts need evaluation. A win is a dopamine hit, an adrenaline rush, and a builder of self-esteem. This is not the phony self-esteem of the late-20th-century educational system, but the original idea. Self-esteem is built via the knowledge that achievements have been reached and positive behaviors and traits have been developed.

Failing to meet a goal is useful. As it is said, no ruler measures a table without the table measuring the ruler as well. When a goal is missed, was it an appropriate goal? This should cause reflection on how one views one's abilities at the time. If missed, why was it missed? One must be honest with this evaluation. The source of failure reveals areas for improvement or weaknesses that one may not be aware of having. From failures, one launches new victories.

Seeking help with crafting goals is appropriate. Teachers, bosses, or coaches have all met many more people due to their exposure within their fields. It is likely they have seen people with the exact profile or strengths and weaknesses that you may have. They can help not just set good goals, but goals to push you. Some people have an overabundance of confidence, but many are uncertain what they are capable of in not just the moment, but the near future.

Of course, goals would be eschewed by our culture. There is a chance for failure! We hide failure and never want anyone to feel the pain or shame of failing. All of life is designed for comfort and avoidance of displeasure. This starts at birth. This is why some children's sports leagues do not keep score. Many people rail against the idea of participation trophies, yet they never think who the trophy is for. Is that trophy for the kid who knows he did not place or knows that he was last, or is it for the parent who does not want to think his or her child is bad at anything? This is society-wide and starts young. This only creates situations where entities cannot handle adversity and the first real brush with failure destroys a soul. The first bit of criticism shatters these glass people.

Nassim Taleb writes often of the problem of how smoothing outcomes and denying any adversity only sets up the organism or entity for massive failure. It is the idea of hormesis, where the small, regular exposures to irritants and challenges strengthens an entity. A daily little dose of arsenic can help one develop a tolerance to it. Victorian women took arsenic for a paler complexion, but nobles and sovereigns knew a little exposure could protect them from an assassin's poisoning attempt. Controlled burns can prevent major forest fires. Cold showers can jolt the body's metabolism. This is not just found in nature. While Taleb's focus is on financial systems, we can see this in our peers' mental and emotional profiles.

The soft, comfortable modern man will complain of back pains, knee pains or leg pain. It just creeps up on him in age. We are literally being coddled to death. Try sitting on a hard floor with your back straight. Sleep on a floor for a few days. You anticipate pain and discomfort. The opposite happens. Your body reacts to the natural situation. Man was not bred to sleep on soft pillows and mattresses. Through eons, the body was adapted to firm, hard surfaces, setting up camps on grasslands on the steppe or in the forest. Sleep on the floor and discover your body feels better, your back is in greater alignment, and those aches and pains in your hips and knees disappear. It is a nightly reset or an eight-hour hormesis session. One will begin to see the monk sitting on a rock not as a masochist, but as a man avoiding the siren song of comfort.

Any of the skills or ways in which you want to develop will need mile markers to measure your progress. These do not need to be Excel sheets with refined numbers to hit or skills to master. Many track athletes have small reminders of their goals. A common one is the piece of paper with a goal or three listed and maybe a picture to remind them of what they are seeking or a moment they triumphed, maybe even failed. Maybe you have seen this. Each night, the runner goes to bed seeing the numbers. Every morning, he wakes up seeing the same numbers. These are his goals. Maybe his friends know them. These do not have to be shared with others. Few if any will know how those goals stared back at him when he lied in bed thinking about an upcoming race. They stare at him in his sleep. He does not need the paper there because they are burned in his mind, but he does so to have proof that the goals were set. At the end of a season or year, only he knows if he met his goals. With a runner or swimmer, the goals are times, and the clock never lies. At the end of that year, it is not the numbers staring at him. It is the man at the beginning of the journey looking at him.

This is for all men and in all endeavors. There should be no fear in failing and no over-exuberance in succeeding. Goals can be tiered and for any realm of your life. Facing challenges will become easier as you amass wins and learn from failures. The steady flow of feedback in your exercises will help ground you as you advance through life. You will not be one of those men asking "what do I do now" and wondering where you stand in life. There will be no rush into poor decisions to catch up to others. Measuring yourself against the acts and status of others will never leave you satisfied and forever enslave you to others' desires.

CHAPTER 2

Are you so confident in your raw intelligence that you feel you know everything? This thinking permeates society. Remember that Socrates said, "I know that I know nothing." How do you know what you know? Through self-study, or from someone else? In your studies, learn about the men that have written what you read. Can you trust them? We are taught not to notice patterns, which is to be mindless. Trust the patterns you see with your eyes and hear with your ears. Not from electronics, but in the real world, unfiltered truth. For too long, we have been conditioned to defer to an outside source for interpretation and information. The ability to manipulate has grown in scope and sophistication. Take back the duty to understand.

Seek truth in the time-tested. Knowledge that has helped your ancestors survive is now denied and mocked by charlatans and clowns. The world's history of thought can be accessed in the palm of your hand. It only needs your touch to be retrieved.

But do not rely solely on yourself for all decisions. No man lives alone. Seek the wisdom of the ages, and seek experts in your circle. You do not have to follow their advice, but you must listen. Maintain humility as you grow wiser. As you accumulate knowledge, you are reminded with each new lesson that just yesterday you were not as enlightened.

Seeking a new skill often directs us to teachers. Seeking the refinement of one's soul and mind is the same. It is not a shame to emulate and confer with a role model or aspirational ideal. These hierarchical relationships are normal. How can you expect to be a father, a boss, or a leader if you do not know what it is to emulate and learn from another? No man can do this alone. Other men seek the path in our mad time. You may enlighten them and they you in return.

Men don't learn from talking. Endless talking is for women to commiserate and share their pain. Men see, act, and react. They practice and repeat. Consider how a son may know that his father was an athlete, and talk to him about trying a sport. The son has heard stories or seen pictures of his father playing this sport, but he does not quite believe it yet. Then the father shows the son, and his skills are revealed. The son may appear confused, as these are powers he never truly knew his father to possess. The stories become real, and an example is now present. The son knows the possibility is real for him, in his time.

For all men, there are two others who have shaped his mind. First is the man that doubted him. The man who never let a moment pass without denigration. The man who mocked him. All men have this figure in their past. It may have been a rival or bully. Worse, it may have been a friend or family member that betrayed his natural role. The memory of this negative man fuels the anger and drive to overcome obstacles. Every swing of a hammer is to break that man's face. Each piece of praise from a contemporary is to drown out that insulting figure. Every achievement is to silence that doubter.

This fuel can burn a man up, which is why there are two men. The second man is the man who believed in him. The man who praised and encouraged him. Each small achievement was catalogued as if for a future hagiography. This was the man who said, "You don't have to work at it, we have to work at it." The memory of this man fuels the determination and steels the soul to see things through to the end. This is the loving spirit that makes us not just determined men, but good leaders.

All men are driven by proving the first man wrong and the second man right. How many listless, directionless men are out there? Odds are they are missing one of these men, sometimes both.

Contemporary times find young men raised by mothers only, relegating fathers to a weekend role as if scheduled into a boy's life. They go to schools where 70 percent of primary teachers are women. If this was your life, it should make you angry. It should steel your soul to make sure it does not happen to the young men in your family.

Today, a young man of 18 is lucky to have had one man in his life to emulate. Who are most left following? Random men in their personal sphere, as sorted by status, and figures in popular media. Recognize that with every relationship, you may find a man seeking someone to believe in him. The smallest encouragements can alter lives.

The problem of boys without fathers is eternal. Our classics often revolve around orphaned sons. There is a passage after Hector's death in *The Iliad* that speaks to the pain of the fatherless son:

"A fatherless son is cut off from the friends of his childhood. He goes about with his head hanging down and his cheeks wet with tears, and when in his need, he comes where the friends of his father are feasting and plucks at one's cloak or another's tunic, someone out of pity holds out his cup for a moment, just long enough to wet the child's lips but leave his palate still dry."

We now have a mass of young men who have grown up with their heads hung low, never knowing their father. Even the slightest moments spent with these children can change their lives. It will never replace the lost feast, but one can offer moments sharing one's cup.

Beyond the immediate, we should seek to emulate those who have come before us. Modern media substitutes new stories, pushing new values to replace the old heroes of your culture. One of the greatest media lies is that reading fiction is a joy because no one is trying to sell you anything. It is a lie because in every character, in every situation, and in every choice, values and ideals are being framed as good or bad. There is a right choice, and the author or storyteller makes sure you know which is which. There is a reason ancient myth and religion intertwined. The storytellers and priests wanted your people to know what was right and wrong, what behaviors to emulate, and what choices to make.

There are few if any memorable contemporary stories because this is a disposable society run by a largely foreign hive mind with values hostile to your own flourishing. These values are always changing, making last season's virtues passé, and even making them this season's sins.

These media makers craft archetypes for people to pattern their lives on that further their own social goals. The smart kid is always weaker than the powerful kid, but magically, his intelligence wins the day. These mythmakers do not want to show that the strong are often smart and the weak dumb. They want people to stay in prescribed roles and not stray or challenge the manicured version of good. Their needs are often at odds with yours or the healthy development of your people.

Learn your people's myths. Do you know even your own family's story? Our contemporary culture shuts the door on the past and discourages this examination. Study your family lines. Your name has a meaning: discover it. Go through your line and find the ancestor to emulate. Travel to their land, see the world as they saw it. When you look out on their land, know that they planted, built, killed, and died for you.

Your existence is atop a pile of bones. Those bones are made up of the family that endured for you. Those bones include those of others that they fought for you. Those bones are made up of the animals that they hunted for sustenance for you. Honor their sacrifice. Do not forget that you are the end result of their efforts. Become a part of the house that is your name.

Contribute your stone to the glorious tradition that has been bequeathed to you. Be the caretaker for the next generation. Become the model for those of the next generation. Teach the next generation about your ancestors. Teach them about the role models from your childhood. Did someone fight in a war or build a home? Was one a carpenter, painter, tradesman, or artist? Did someone plan cities and build roads?

Art and tradition are not simply created, but must be maintained and cultivated so that the next generation understands their meaning. Did your family have traditions? Does your culture have traditions? Have you seen old photographs of your family going hunting, playing music, or wearing certain clothing? Why did this stop?

It is rarely money. It is sometimes time, but it is always energy. The one with the energy to continue a tradition will find the time and money. Time is the weakest of excuses for not eating a traditional dish or meal. Think of how little time people had prior to modern conveniences. Replace an hour of mindless watching or scrolling with the revival of a family tradition or creation of a new one.

People do not find the energy for traditions because they are not a priority. They have no value for the past because their mind is so focused on media consumption and connectivity in the now. With no past links, they will leave a barren wasteland for the future.

Food held a spot in your culture for a reason. The junk food of this junk culture has destroyed that connection for a reason, but you can restart traditions. Your family practiced them through war, famine, and disease, or created new ones in response to hardship. In an era of chaos, you too can start traditions. The holiday table that presents chips, salsa, and bits of refined sugar once displayed other foods. Find out what they were. Understand why they were a part of your family's celebrations.

Your grandmother made sauerkraut every New Year's Day for the family. Do you know why? It was for good luck in the new year. She made it herself, but even buying sauerkraut on that day would honor her and the women who came before. Or maybe you can find the old recipe and start anew. This might feel forced to you, but to a child, even a new tradition will always be a part of their life. Each bite of that food will bring a memory and a feeling. Our sense of smell is even more closely linked with memory. Who made this before? With whom have I shared this? These are my people. These are those I love.

CHAPTER 3

You are willing to learn. This is good. Even in our era of madness, there is a prestige to being learned. You will not learn for others to pat you on the head and feed you a biscuit. That is a child's approach. The applause of others is nothing compared to the satisfaction of gathered wisdom. Not many men can be a warlord or warrior in our open-air asylum, but you can be a wise man.

Be careful not to fall into the fads of the smart set as framed by the media. Do not love science, understand science. Do not just parrot the headline. Do notice the oddity of the coordinated new facts that contradict the same institutions' old facts. Seek the source. Seek reality. It shall be your guide. With contemporary technology, there is no hindrance to becoming a scholar. This is the age of the autodidact. Whatever knowledge you seek, whatever skill you wish to learn is at your fingers. You do not have to travel far for the information or for the wisdom of scholars. It is right there, waiting to be found.

These old masters shout out to you in voices. They fought similar battles, both external and internal. They offer you advice. They offer solutions. They share warnings. They are men just as you are, but men who could also read and write in Greek and Latin.

Recently, the entire chattering class of society has tried to rationalize away an army of intelligent political amateurs. They first accused these amateurs of being robots, then Russian agents, then some other kind of agents. Every cliché and false argument had been destroyed by a kernel of men armed only with knowledge they learned in their spare time.

Study does not come naturally to anyone. Even the genius you knew in childhood hit a point where they could no longer simply absorb facts, but had to learn to study and think. We all had to learn to study. To start down the path of studying is to humble yourself before another. You are dedicating time, attention, and mindfulness to another's words. Do not give up on studying. Do not give up so easily. Have you read for 21 days straight? If you cannot do a simple task such as read for 21 days straight, how can you master a new skill? How can you master yourself?

Devote a period of time each day to reading and studying. The subject matter may change and the reading material may rotate, but dedicate the time each day. Study and learn. Put away your phone. Turn off your television. While they can be tools in your educational journey, they are often time sinks. Every moment wasted on them is a moment taken from your life employed for the ends of another.

If you are an American, you waste on average six hours a day on television. If you are awake for 16 hours a day, that is nearly half of your waking life. One can fit an entire other life into the amount of time Americans watch television.

Studying takes discipline in an undisciplined society. It takes the ability to quiet the mind and not lunge for the phone after three pages of reading. When you study, do not approach it as a chore. Devote an hour to learning and reading. Do not be an intellectual, but be a man that studies and learns.

An intellectual in our era is a man who assumes an identity and pays attention to the proper fashions for that role. The intellectual with horn-rimmed glasses will tell you any fool knows the Earth revolves around the sun but does not know why. That intellectual has spent more time selecting his glasses, his haircut, and maintaining proper orientation to the zeitgeist than he has looking into why the Earth orbits the sun. He does not know. An hour of study could reveal the gravitational tug of war between everything in the solar system that comes to balance at the center of gravity. The horn-rimmed glasses fellow would pick up his phone and locate an article on Wikipedia, but it would fail him. He would need to actually look into this.

His claim to intelligence is the proper graduate degree. It is his certificate to wrap himself in, hiding his lack of mental curiosity or prowess. The degree covers his hollow claim to intelligence. This man has outsourced his knowledge to an external source. He has not bothered to look into this. He has placed his mind at the mercy of a digital curator. He does not study, yet considers himself learned.

Once the daily hour studying is a part of your routine, it has become a part of your mindset and daily system. There is no fitting study into your day because your day is not a complete day without study. You will seek things to fill that hour. Once this has been accomplished, it will be easy to dedicate oneself to study every day for a specific subject.

Be careful not to let writers think for you. Schopenhauer warned of the men that spent all of their time reading, allowing others to think for them. Read, learn, and reflect. Take what you read and consider the immediate world around you. Do not be afraid to sit, smoke, or drink and think. Contemporary man complains about the hectic pace of society, yet fills all of his time with distracting noise and entertainment. He reaches for his phone after 60 seconds of silence. In a generation, the American attention span shrunk to that of a fish. Tell someone this and he will shrug and move on without thinking how he does it to himself.

Modern man cannot even drive from his house to his place of work without turning on the radio to fill his car with noise. It is not to stimulate his mind or learn something new. The noise is turned on to fill the silence. In a twenty minute drive, they will flip between music stations or talk radio. Ask them afterwards what they listened to, and they will have a cursory understanding of what was spoken. They just need to hear something. Juvenile songs about sex. The possible shuffling of athletes between teams. Some political issue in which they have no control and possibly no interest. It is a system of noise that soothes them from thinking for just twenty minutes. Men cannot be alone with their thoughts. They are not empty vessels. It is more that they have forgotten to reflect and contemplate life. Possibly, they are afraid of what their minds may lead them towards.

Mathematics, language, and history are a foundation. They can fill an infinite number of hours to study. They can inspire the mind to think on its own and understand the world around it. Mathematics is the foundation for modern science. The ability to prove and disprove with mathematics is the philosophical basis of science. If you can measure and predict with great accuracy, you have quantifiable proof that your beliefs and assumptions are true.

Math has high practical use, for learning to be quick with figures can help with estimating solutions to problems at hand. This feeds one's competence, confidence, and judgment. If one can feel comfortable with one's estimates, a proposed solution inspires more confidence.

Language is the means to understand the past and understand foreign cultures. It is impossible to understand a language without learning who created it, who uses it, and what were the land and struggles that formed it. History is not merely reading about an event or a people. Do not fall into the modern trap of a few Internet searches and one book purchase to pretend to be an expert. This is the shallow dilettante's approach. What you will build is the three-minute party monologue about a subject. Often these monologues are framed so that a contemporary political point can be served. To reduce history, events, and people down to a three-minute talk is a disservice to everyone. The listener learns nothing. The topic is not given its proper appreciation. The speaker receives a faux sense of superiority and knowledge. These spiels are more declarations of adherence to religious orthodoxy.

Far worse than the Google-and-one-book expert is the man that starts every discussion with, "I saw a documentary…" You bring up the complex web of interests, bad incentives, and problems of choice that lead to the obesity epidemic. Their response is, "I saw a documentary," and progressive regurgitation follows. You discuss the problem of medical regulation and how the problem is not really the uninsured as much as the red tape that affects the insured. Their response is, "I saw a documentary," and progressive regurgitation follows. You mention the dearth of documentaries on communist-led genocides. Their response is, "There is no documentary," and they mention a Holocaust documentary. You also recall from prior chats how they discuss scrolling on their phone while watching videos, revealing the shallow exposure they have to many topics. They are not just straitjacketed by their ideological beliefs, but in their methods for learning.

This is a straitjacket that affects all who are subject to the media and academic memeplex. It is possible to break its grasp. History is best studied in a people's own words. To read a people in their own words often requires the need to learn their language. One cannot know a people unless you know their history, their poetry, their insults and folklore. Take advantage of the technology available. As with any subject, dedicate time within one's day to consistently refine your knowledge. The man that listens to 20 minutes of drugged out men warbling over guitars can listen to 20 minutes of German-language instruction or Japanese haikus. The men of your line often knew multiple languages. The leading men of history knew several languages to speak with contemporary peers and to read the classics in the original texts. If you do not know a language of another culture and seek to learn about it, all texts will be filtered by the mind of the translator. Seek knowledge not just for practical application, but for development of the mind and soul.

Challenge oneself to create processes and systems for thinking and approaching problems. Learn the challenges others faced and how they resolved them. Do not consider your small studies to be insignificant. Many credentialed graduate students read an ever-narrowing scope of books to create dissertations read by a handful of people and journal articles read by none. Look at the humanities PhD scholar now serving at the feet of an old professor seeking the blessing of tenure track. He snorts a laugh at the thought of the medieval or even Dark Ages monk. Odd vows to superstitions and a hierarchy of older men: what a funny little mental movie. They laugh to hide the ancient monks' wonderful work. That monk transcribed the classics and wrote pieces himself that are read a millennium later. The humble monk's work allowed the flowering of Europe and growth of a civilization.

The modern humanities PhD is a monk in form, but not in spirit. He contributes nothing. His works, mostly derivative, are not read by anyone. The humanities PhD chuckles at the thought of a monks' fast or Lenten observations while openly telling everyone they can that they do not consume any animal products. The old Catholic scholar from a millennium ago gave up his meat on Fridays, but the good humanities PhD proves his holiness by forgoing meat for a lifetime. The credentialed scholar dances to the warped tune of a guild that is corrupted by its privilege and power.

As you study, you will notice patterns to life and history. Ideas of truth and objectivity will form, will feel almost as tangible as the paper you hold. Those who promote relativism, those who cry about noticing patterns, are often those who earn a credential by studying nothing and producing things no one will read or value. Their argument is merely a volley to keep them and their ilk entrenched in power. The more you study, the more you will see that same mechanism used.

Studying and learning is not meant to be a solitary adventure. There are others that read and study. Bring up your reading, bring up your discoveries, and discuss the lessons with others. Be the caretaker for your history and culture. This means not just learning, but educating, setting others along the path to learning. They live in this same fallen society, and we all need each other in this endeavor.

While being smart is elevated, few follow through and attain wisdom. Many study with no practice in challenging what they have learned. The self-styled intellectual that buys the right clothes and has a bachelor's degree, does he read more books than the New England millworker of 75 years ago? Many contemporary men read far more than the fashionable intellectual. Engage with these private scholars.

When more learn and study the same thing, actions can be coordinated. Private organizing allows for open discussions. This coordination makes it is easier to communicate in public without being blunt; the esoteric opens up as a possibility. The group can hone in on valuable traditions and collectively carry them forward.

CHAPTER 4

The men of your line were active men. Not all were warriors, but many plowed, mined, built, and used their bodies. You stand at the tip of that evolutionary path. Do you stand strong on top of the mountain of bones, or do you hide in the shadow of those skulls?

Those men that carved a life out of the land were no different physically from you. Their body is your body. Their strengths are your strengths. Their weaknesses are your weaknesses. We can use their wisdom of how to strengthen the body and mind, as well as what continues to be discovered.

What is your aesthetic? Do you even know how you appear? Do you care? The calls for not considering aesthetics are from those who are ugly, who celebrate the ugly, or who want to drag all into the ugly. The human body is not meant to be overinflated skin filled with fat. Those who encourage this want you sluggish and slow. They want you sick and limping through life.

Look at the men who shuffle like defeated tribesmen, shoulders hunched forward, heads down, eyes down. Everything curling inward as if hiding from the world. They take up as little space as possible, afraid to own the ground they walk on. They are as helots waiting for the strike from their masters. Men who move like bugs afraid of the light roll their eyes at eating meats and cheeses. Those are not healthy per the credentialed experts. They eat processed soy and vegetarian meat substitutes. They hold their heads high eating their recommended diet of grains and vegetables. They might as well eat grass, like cattle. These foods weaken them, yet they eat them because they were told them they were healthy.

They turn their faces from eating foods of power. Kidney, calf's brain, liver, and shellfish they avoid, but eat third-world concoctions made with rancid oils and half-digestible exotic grains. Their food is exotic, so it is preferable to the steppe meals that fueled the conquering of a continent. They recoil at calf's brain fried in butter but gleefully seek mystery meat from the back of food trucks. They choose novelty over knowledge.

They do not eat food for power but for the possibility of one extra day. Rather than live with *thumos,* they simply want to exist. The three Thai restaurants in your city all have the same menu. Maybe you even eek out an extra two or three years by eating like a South American peasant. What does it do for you? You live a life resembling a fearful mole in the city. Three extra years of that is of no value.

These men give in to the standards of someone else's weights and measurements. These standards change and contradict themselves over time. Eggs were good, then bad, and now good. Studies about fats now contradict a generation of official messaging. The universities took bribes to conduct studies that molded certain recommendations.

Forget what these men eat; look at how they eat. They nibble on foreign food, detached from their cultures' traditions. They eat quickly, forgetting to savor the meal as if it might be their last. When working, they eat out of plastic dishes at their desks. Heads lurching forward and down, as if a weight presses on their neck. Even in a park, they eat mouthfuls while glancing at their screens, unaware of their environment. These are men moving as if they are afraid of death visiting them at any moment, ignorant that this is always the case.

The media blessing that something can extend one's life is the justification for the most self-destructive rationalizations of these bugmen. The priest has given the blessing for an act, therefore to engage in it, no matter how ridiculous, is a good thing. What if those extra three years is spent in dementia or beset by illnesses and immobile? They deny a lived life with risks and joy to maximize their monk existence. Death comes. There is no avoiding it. The only question is if death will be noble or not.

The system shows you images of fit men, yet there are few consequences for the overwhelming number of men who are not fit. It does the same with women, but with the added perversion that to attempt to look fit or to prefer fit women is a form of oppressive shaming.

Look at the men in old photos. There may have been the fat man with a nickname involving his large appearance, but he was one man. Most are lean, fit, and look strong, maybe even hungry. Look around you in a public space. Most live a soft life with soft bodies and soft minds. Men wishing to recreate the physical struggle attend designated fitness facility centers to trick the body into developing as intended. They do not sharpen the mind nor the body even with this knowledge. This is as much from a fear of failure as from inertia.

To be a man is to develop strength. It is our purpose. Warrior, protector, defender; these are traditional roles that we were designed to fulfill. Respect is accorded to a man who handles himself in a battle, mental or physical. A man who is physically fit naturally has others defer to him.

Two out of three men are overweight. Look at your family and circle of friends. Is there a pattern? On which piece of the pie chart are you? Walking the earth 20 or 40 pounds overweight is a series of steps. It does not happen overnight, or else we would see media reports about the phenomenon of midnight body ballooning. Each man sitting there grossly overweight made a thousand small choices to get to that point. He sat when he could stand. He chose to ride rather than walk. He chose to walk rather than run. He had one more serving. He had one more handful of chips. He had one cookie at three o'clock. After years, the doctor tells him he has a problem and he wonders how he got there. He lacked mindfulness. He did not pay attention to his immediate choices. He lost awareness and was mindlessly consuming and slogging through his days. That man watched as the man in the mirror looked back at him in worse and worse condition, but he failed to act.

This is not all men. We all know the old lion that sees young men joking around at a barbecue or holiday meal. He rises out of his chair and walks over to the young guys. He shares a joke, maybe offers commentary. But before he leaves, he shakes their hands. It's not a handshake as much as a test of grip. The older man knows his strength and knows these young men view him as past his prime. He squeezes their hands and notes their reactions. He might even laugh a bit if they can keep pressure or match him. The old man walks off smiling.

The next day, the younger men will complain about their hands or wrists hurting. They'll laugh that it was the old man's grip. They will all respect his strength. The handshake is important. It is your introduction and first impression of other men. Consider it a ritual to work on to set the tone of your leadership. No matter the accomplishments, a man with a weak handshake will be remembered as weak. Grab the hand firmly and squeeze down to your palm. Make eye contact. Do not look away as you shake hands, as making eye contact is a sign of confidence. Prizefighters talk of the meaning of the stare-down pre-fight. Who breaks their gaze first? Who breaks the seriousness first? It is a sign of willpower. To not hold a stare is to signal you cannot stand an attack.

The man who is fit sets himself apart from the crowd. This is a fallen society. Form is now following function. It is not just the level of fitness. Even the novice notices that after working out his walk changes. His posture is different. His handshake is firmer. His back stands straighter. This can happen after a month. A body you never knew you had begins to form. It responds in ways you did not consider or expect.

Firmer handshakes and sitting straighter happened without a conscious effort to work on any single item. This was your body developing into the figure you were meant to have. As one's legs strengthen, one's gait will change. Without consciously affecting any change, the walk becomes one of confidence. This leads to conscious self-respect for your status as a man.

The self-esteem peddled today is about feeling good regardless of achievements. This is because society does not understand the difference between earning self-respect through one's actions and earning approval of an outside authority. Self-esteem through accomplishment, even just moving more weight, is a powerful factor in an individual's mental health.

Voices call this yearning for optimal function and form toxic masculinity. It is not toxic to your life. It is part of your life. It is toxic to their worldview and to their hold over your mind.

The man who is fit is not just reliable in a pinch, but more assured and confident of himself. His body joins his mind in being ready for any challenge. The men who set out with Columbus into an empty ocean did not do so in a slovenly state. "It is so hard to begin. It is so hard to stick to it." The voices give you excuses before you even start. Some of them do not want you to improve.

Others ask, "Why would he do that?" It is not just with carving one's physique, but any endeavor that stands out. They do not ask to hear why. They are just voicing disapproval.

Think of the January gym attendee. They know they are weak or flabby. They know they need to change. There is some awareness that they need a new direction. They say that this January they are going to join a gym and get in shape. The cultural phenomenon is so well known that this is incorporated into gym marketing. It is known that by February most all of them are gone.

If you see an obese man in the gym struggling on a treadmill or with a weight, do not mock him. Encourage him. At some moment, we all have been the new gym attendee. We all have been the out-of-shape man. We have all been the man placing light weights on bars to lift. We all have been the tired, weak man struggling not to look horrible at the new gym. Help your fellow brother return in February and feel that he is a member of the club.

Why do these men wait for January? Even with their decision to do it, why did they wait to start in January? Do not delay. Start at the moment. Start small. Reflect. Conditioning started in haste will not go nearly as well as a process with planning. Start doing some activity each day. Walk at lunch. Walk before work or class. Walk after work or class. Incorporate some activity into your life. Activity will become something you seek rather than something you have to do. Sampling different sports, movements, and activities will develop all of your muscles.

You don't even need a gym. Three simple, foundational compound movements are the pull-up, the push-up, and the squat. What is the excuse when a doorframe pull-up bar costs as much as a case of beer?

Sets of pull-ups develop your back. Push-ups strengthen your chest. How few sets does it take for you to reach 100 push-ups? How many can you do to failure? Look at military standards for these movements. Reach them. Beat them. Perform two pull-ups and 50 push-ups in a few minutes and you are already ahead of most men. Perform squats with milk jugs full of water. Sit-ups and crunches can be done anywhere.

For the cost of a few trips to fast food joints, one can buy a sparring glove set and jump rope. One can throw a punch in a living room. A roommate, a friend or a son can work with you. Feel your shoulders after throwing one hundred punches. You will sweat after jumping rope for five minutes. You will be miles ahead of the crowd simply by starting this at home. You will want to do more.

There is no need to start molding one's body with a fancy gym membership. Build towards it so that it is a new level of activity. There is a system that works for every body type. There are systems that play to your strengths. There are styles that challenge you. All will provide a spark in your synapses. All will offer incremental challenges. All offer the choice for better health and greater strength.

Do not become a product of a set of sequences like an android. Consider your work, your life, and your daily functions, not just the aesthetic results. Be careful of creating a mechanical routine. This afflicts even the confident gym enthusiast. The young man who pushes iron joins his uncle on a hunt. He feels far stronger than his older uncle. He can load the truck up quicker and with ease. The uncle and nephew stay up setting the morning's kits. They stay up late smoking cigars and enjoying drinks. They tell stories until 2AM.

Before dawn, the old uncle wakes up his nephew. The young man is startled. His head is still foggy from the spirits and smoke. He was a pure body, trained in the gym and free of pollutants. They set out in the dark, trudging through snow. The young man bounds up over some obstacles and removes others with ease. But the hiking weakens him. The mountains and snow reveal that he lacks the endurance, pacing, and persistence of the older hunter.

Once in place, the older hunter rests, and enjoying the crisp air. He reads and naps. The young man cannot. His mind is not at ease. He has strength, but doesn't know how to use it for a lifetime of marches. The strength he has developed is not fully meshed into his bearing.

One does not need to be a professional bodybuilder, but the statues of classical Greece and Rome do conjure up the image of man at full potential. All victory has come to those who looked the best or destroyed the best. This is evolution at its more raw. Hercules killed the many-headed hydra with fire and the sword. Men cleared the forest with fire and the axe. Strength cleared the land and fed the community.

Ancient men raided towns and made off with the young women, who resisted through kicks, bites, and scratches. Can you carry a bride over the short distance of a home's threshold? You do not need to lower yourself to contemporary standards. Your standards should be the timeless and eternal.

A man of physical strength can destroy his enemies. A man of mental strength can outwit his enemies. Men of strength, whether mental or physical, are men at their fullest potential. These men striving for the peak of physical aesthetics will attract followers. No one follows a weak, soft man. Men seek an iron will and iron physique. Like iron, your training is born of study, fire, and hammering. You pound and beat your body to mold it into the proper form to strike at a decadent world.

Other men will see strength and want to be like a strong man. Women will gravitate towards strong men because power is the ultimate aphrodisiac. No woman fantasizes about a weakling. She will consider a weak man a fellow woman and treat him as one, a companion for shopping, coffee, and chatting about TV shows. Maybe he'll get a hug when she leaves. She has turned him into a dickless boyfriend, and a dickless man is just another girlfriend, below even her gay friend for status. She can brag about her gay friend and get approval for her open-mindedness. Weak men have forgotten that they do not need such women in their lives.

A man who seeks physical strength in these chaotic times is rebelling against the conditioning that encourages hedonism and avoidance of pain. A strong man is a threat. Strength means independence and the ability to take care of one's concerns.

Have you noticed how the overlords who rush into action the moment any contamination is found in our food or water will turn a blind eye to chemicals and pills that feminize men? Residual estrogen from birth control pills in public water? No concern. Plastic in children's toys and cups that mimics estrogen? No concern. Soy in nearly every food? No concern. Testosterone-lowering Ritalin and Adderall? School staples for boys.

These chemicals, foods, and pills all feminize men, yet this is not seen as harmful by the authorities. They want men weak and feminized so that they clamor for a third party to provide security. Strong men are superfluous, their roles outsourced, but this will come to an end. Strong, confident men stand out more than ever, and as chaos begets trouble, they will be valued as they always are when survival is at stake.

CHAPTER 5

One trains the mind and body for a purpose. It is not mere excellence and perfection. Violence is part of a man's life. You train for the fight. For many, this is a sanitized world. For polite society, conflict is avoided. Agreeableness is the desired trait. No friction, no fighting.

It starts from birth. Look at children's cartoons. Your grandfather watched Tom and Jerry or Bugs and Daffy attempt to kill one another for ten minutes straight. You watched robots and monsters fight galactic battles. Your child watches Daniel Tiger overcome his anxiety about playing soccer.

Some men spend a lifetime wondering how they stack up. A lifetime of talk and thought is nothing compared to the first time you must hit or be hit. Were you hit as a child? Then you already know. You know that one strike is just one hit. The body reacts per evolution. The nervous system alters one's heart rate to accelerate. Nerves signal pain. Adrenaline flows. Pain. Maybe a momentary numbness. What matters is what you do next. The long fights of Hollywood movies seldom exist in real life. The next few seconds after the spark of the fight settle it.

Fight or flight. Fight or submit. Defend territory. Defend your loved ones. Defend honor. Defend yourself. These are the patterns. A failure to defend any of these is a failure to perform the basic duties of man. Did anyone even teach you how to throw a punch? Teach the young this basic skill.

The Meiji Restoration would not have happened if the shoguns could have defended Japan from the Americans. All of that power came with responsibility. Their power depended on this duty. They failed. The charade was exposed. Their power over other elite men was gone because their claim to duties and rights was false.

Men thirst for a fight, and it is expressed in their love for simulated violence. They implicitly vocalize their disdain for our sedentary society. They simply want to fight, kill, hunt, and defend. They seek these opportunities in all of their entertainment. They shoot soldiers in first-person perspective video games. They enjoy the vicious fighting of an MMA telecast. They talk of their zombie apocalypse plan. The urge to fight is hidden in plain sight.

Some will question why these men have not signed up for the military. Some do, but millions do not. What wars would they fight? Is it for home and family? The wars of choice our elites select for us are packaged, marketed, and wrapped up in patriotism, but there is no struggle for our people. These conflicts are handpicked for the goals of the empire, not the goals of your tribe. These war marketers shy away from saying a conflict is a civilizational battle.

There is no longer any outlet for officially sanctioned righteous violence. A fighting man would go to prison for defending his hometown against drug dealers or patrolling the border to shoot interlopers, and he would get a longer sentence if the court considered it a hate crime.

Some men run away from the internal struggle with their soul. How could they struggle against an enemy? Some are afraid of the slightest physical or social loss. The only loss that stirs their soul is on their 401k balance or a fantasy football league.

To win every battle is ideal, but not necessary. An aggressor will be foiled if they find that resistance is enough to change the calculus. Consider the history of duels. Attacking the honor of another came with consequences, the ultimate being death. It was not the willingness to kill that mattered, but the willingness to risk your life to defend your honor. Shots could be thrown or wasted, but to have stood at ten paces and faced the barrel of a gun was the proof of one's honor. One may not kill for it, but one would die for it.

Even for a victorious man, to enter the duel came with consequences. Why was one's honor even considered in threat? To place oneself in the position to have to put one's life at risk for one's honor meant that poor choices had been made to expose oneself.

Look around at male honor today. No brotherhood. Sniping and insults that have moved from the physical realm to the digital. Even the violence in our urban hellscapes has devolved from hand-to-hand combat to drive-by shootings. Youths defend supposed honor, for they hold nothing else of value, by shooting at one another's homes, basketball courts, or porches, catching innocents caught in the crossfire. Their women and children suffer the fatal blows that should be dealt the hood warriors. This is a symptom of lost honor among all men.

Contemporary man cannot understand dying for a trait to which they assign no value. Cowardly or simply autistic, they cannot comprehend how anyone could assign value to the trait. Modern man believes in an invisible force like gravity, but cannot consider the intangible feeling of honor. The Western man devoid of honor will claim superiority, laugh, and mock the corruption of Russian or Chinese politicians and businessmen. They fail to see the honoring of a contract between interests. They also fail to see donations to politicians and cushy jobs for them when out of office are the exact same bribery they mock elsewhere, only formalized and blessed with legality.

They mock the Iranian officials and citizens that seek guidance from a black-turbaned jurist-theologian while waiting for a decision from black-robed Harvard trained jurists to bless gay marriage. A focus on legality and writing obscures the man that enforces it. Western men want to remove themselves from duty and responsibility. They want to remove the human element. Forget right or honorable; if it is written down somewhere, it is legal and acceptable. Honor and shame cannot be written away or into existence.

The nominal father dare not tell his daughter to show restraint and guard her honor. No, he feels like a good father while allowing a 14-year-old to date and play the field. He acquiesces despite having noticed the poor romantic decisions of his sisters, aunts, and friends. The father has abdicated, the throne sits empty. The role is still required, but no one performs it, leading to chaos.

The father submits to the animal spirits of a 14-year-old girl. Any man she likes is allowed to walk through his home and remove his daughter for the evening. Father must get back to his fantasy football draft. If she has a brother, he may instinctively object. He might tell his mom and dad that the suitor is not right. He is too young to see that the role of protective brother is not valued or needed any longer. The parents will chide him, the father might tell him to cool down or lay off, because the chastity of young women in the home is not of anyone's concern. It is the current year, young man!

How many pay no mind to their daughter's clothes? How many care not when the police drop her off after finding her somewhere? How many have no sense of the shame or potential shame brought on their homes? They do not care, but for the moment, a permanent reminder of their failure, a new baby, enters the home. Then the household swarms to protect. This is a maternal move. Often, the father is enraged, but his wife tells him they will provide for this new child. This only encourages more dishonorable behavior. Who is watching the babies of young single moms? The grandparents will care for it and raise the bastard child because it is the right thing, the honorable thing to do. A good father helps in this moment. Honor matters then, but it is a fraud. It is a crystal statue that shatters when the smallest of observers knock on it.

"Where were you for the days, week, months and years leading up to that moment," we might ask. *"Where was your honor then?"* No one asks this because it would be rude. Such a comment implies a functioning community with corrective mechanisms, but it would be shouted down in this matriarchal culture that celebrates single mothers.

Maybe 20 years later, it will dawn on the derelict father that one bad decision one evening led to a hard life and dead end for his genetic line. Behind every single mom with a child of a man below her station in life stands a weak or absent father. These men knew what they had to do, but failed. One could hear it in their praise of the television program *To Catch a Predator*. Oh, how the suburban crowd watched it. How they laughed at the sleazy men caught in the trap. How they loved the tall, stern man criticizing the parade of slime seeking sex with the 13-year-old daughters and sons of America. They did not stop to think they were cheering on the avatar of the responsible father, the role they have been avoiding.

Chris Hanson, tall, handsome, and eloquent, delivered rebukes and criticized the scum of contemporary America prowling the Internet for young flesh. He told old men, teachers, immigrants, and eternal bachelors that they were perverted and sick. He told them that their prey did not exist and that they should not even seek them. He chastised them before authorities arrested them. His role was to act as the moral force, judging them and protecting the young. Hanson told the audience what they should have done every weekend with their families. Hanson showed them their failure, how they shirked basic duties passed on for generations.

In this society devoid of honor, the audience did not even grasp this basic lesson. They left their children to be preyed on by others simply because they did not want to fight. What are these men even for, these fathers and brothers and uncles? Having abdicated this protective role, why train for strength and martial prowess? Why prime the mind, body, and soul for duty and conflict? The bugmen do not see a use for any of this. They fail to grasp their reason for existence.

It is a mad world or a sick society, but one where men comply with the feminized norms. Do you doubt it? Some men practically ask their friends to hold them back or they will start swinging. Consider the millions of men who threaten that one day the system will push them to limits. They are always waiting for permission. Consider the millions of young black men who threatened to kill one Floridian if he walked free, yet five years on, he still lives. It did not quite matter as much as they whined that it did. Consider the millions of small interactions that mere decades ago would have created a challenge and fight over honor get brushed off and endured.

Even the instinctual response today is to sue. This is so ingrained in our culture that our pop media mocked the knee-jerk reaction of litigation decades ago. To call in the sanctioned arbiters of fault and justice is the modern man's immediate response to challenge or a severe offense. No one dares knock down the doors of the offending party and seek immediate justice. That is *barbaric*. We are a nation of laws forgetting to check the men behind those laws. Men have been domesticated so quickly to shun all instincts and cry barbaric at the thought of beating someone who has wronged them.

A child is stomped in school. Out of nowhere and for no reason. Eyewitness accounts from other students support the victim. What were the monitors and teachers on watch doing? The school gives poor excuses for not preventing it or breaking up the assault earlier. Parents are angry and the school-assigned cop even states that the family is making a big deal out of this. Photos reveal shoeprints days later. You know this because you see it on a social media feed. The victim's mother goes to social media to cry for sympathy because no one is doing anything. The system does not want to, yet the family still believes in doing something. They have handed over sovereignty and power to an authority that does not care.

What good did all the surveillance technology do for that victim? Where is the victim's father? Where is his agency? What is his power and influence? Where is his circle of family and friends? The perpetrator has a family. In days of old, this would have been settled by the families. Instead, the pity social media post goes up, dad buys his kid a toy, and the world moves on. A familial act of justice would prevent the next stomping for another child, but that is *barbaric*.

This small act goes without response. What does it teach a child? It teaches a child to grow up and threaten to go off if pushed far enough, but to never get around to doing so. Everyone is afraid of defending their territory. They will rely on an authority to do so, despite knowing authorities do nothing. They will vote in a savior. They will call the cops. They will sue.

It will do nothing. No matter the elected authority, the situation on the ground is controlled by men with the will to do so. Tough talk is just talk when you also look over your shoulder before saying the slightest socially dicey phrase or word. This is not all groups and not all men. It is best to learn from them. Does everyone merit your warmth and reassuring smiles? How often do you smile at strangers? Why? Who even told you to do this?

Cops and the legal system are there but after the fact. What piece of paper, like a restraining order or what settlement, like $50,000 in damages, compares to telling your loved one that an offender will not bother them ever again, maybe not walk or chew the same ever again? How does your kid's eyes light up when you say that the judge and jury agreed with them versus when you reveal that their bully's parent will sleep anxiously for weeks? This is not to encourage violence, but to consider the confrontational manner of immediately pushing back on the problems around you.

One of the greatest tricks that the modern world has pulled is convincing people that they can trust in a third party to settle all disputes in a neutral fashion, and that if they did so, they could even end up rich by using the proper channels.

This is a trick. The system has a bias of who-whom. It knows who it wants to protect. Are you in their inner circle? Imagine telling your ancestors about these problems, local and global, and discussing how you are fine with a third party that is nowhere near neutral or fair being the arbiter of justice. They would ask you why any piece of paper would convince a stalker from harming your daughter. They would laugh at the idea of litigation against a delinquent's parent being more satisfying than banging on their door and tearing into them. A teacher has sex with your 13-year-old child still teaches while under investigation, and you are fine with the authorities dragging their feet? Your ancestors would guffaw and shame you.

These were the men that roamed forests for food. They hunted with equipment that gave their prey great odds. They set foot in lands with no guides or maps. They realized that sometimes torches and pitchforks were necessary when grievances to the king would take too long or go unanswered. Your ancestors were men that were not afraid to take action with their own hands, with their brothers and neighbors, and to suffer the consequences. This was their order, their way, and their set of norms.

This is not our way, as we are more civilized. What is civilized about enduring the small cuts or humiliations at the hands of an indifferent system and malicious individuals? We are more cowardly. There are countless other behaviors that we engage in that are uncivilized or degraded from those old days that no amount of legal restraint is going to make up for us to claim superiority. We are mollified. We are pacified. We have been conned into the belief that words on paper mean that the men behind them do not matter.

Deep in our souls, we understand this con. We know it for the fraud that it is no matter the packaging or rivers of words that explain its superiority. We understand honor. As children and even as grown men, many men read stories set on alien planets or with a modern man sent to another time. Suddenly, the opportunity arises for the modern man, comfortable with laws and magistrates, to act in a more primitive mode. The idea of fighting for honor and proving one's mettle is woven into all of these stories that the readers, young and old, project themselves into with their hands gripping the book.

Does the hero shirk from it? Never. There is the momentary questioning of whether he has what it takes, but the hero relishes the chance to use a sword or gun to settle accounts. Oftentimes, this character is a man of our age thrust into a barbaric or supposedly simpler culture or time who has knowledge of our world of laws and procedures, but eschews that for the chance to use the sword and his might to win. He knows that system that he has escaped is a scam. These stories reflect the deep truth known in all of our hearts that the culture of talking it out and negotiated settlements is a culture of lies. Lies will win in that system and persuade just enough of a coalition to agree for the sake of not resorting to violence. The boys and men who read these stories know this truth that cannot be spoken in public and feel this longing that no woman can understand.

Whether a contemporary movie like *Braveheart* or ancient texts, the story is written echoing the words from Agamemnon in *The Iliad:* "Be men, my friends, and stout of heart! Fear nothing in this great clash but dishonor before each other. Of men who shun dishonor, more are saved than slain, but flight is a poor defense and wins no glory of any kind." The civilized world has robbed all men of the opportunity to display the honorable side of their identity with paper and procedures. Those whose hands write on the paper and write the procedures do not have your interests at heart, nor do they even understand what old, dormant feelings lie within you.

Even as you read this, there are scores of people working on creating artificial intelligence. This will allow for efficiency and decision making to streamline our world. It starts small with industrial decisions or even retail store decision-making. The small victories will fund further investment and trustworthy outcomes, encouraging people to hand over more power to the algorithms and AI. Buried in the promise is that artificial intelligence may even perform the hard governance decisions that no one wants to make. Belief in the paper will become belief in the code. Our cowardly society uses consensus to spread the blame for any negative pushback from a decision. No one wants the power to decide the exception. A computer can do it and no one can complain.

It is cowardice and not Stoicism. Stoicism was the practice of enduring the pains and pleasures of life with little reaction. This is the generous interpretation of a philosophy that was born of Greeks who had been conquered by invading barbarians from the north. The Macedonian kings had come down and reduced the glory that was ancient Greece to mere provinces in an empire. The thinkers of the city-states that ruled their lands and enjoyed small empires, whether Athens, Sparta or the later Theban hegemony, were mere subjects of another tribe's empire. This only grew worse as the Romans replaced the Macedonians as new rulers. What better way to cope with this reduction to subjects and hired tutors of the new aristocracy's children than a philosophy of enduring the suffering of the world? Live the life of private virtue and turn inward.

Eventually for the new rulers, it would become a coping mechanism. Stoicism was a bit of coping with the decline of Rome. Marcus Aurelius could push Stoicism as emperor of the peak of the Roman Empire. As emperor at the apogee of the empire, he could see that there were forces even beyond his control. His *Meditations* were a product of a lifetime of learning even his limitations. Used by other Romans, Stoicism was a salve to the damaged egos that nothing a Roman could do that would overcome the wishes of the Empire. Modern man is no Aurelius. Even our leaders are more like the senators and plebeians of old.

It is different for the plebeian. Stoicism leads to passivity. It leads one to feel helpless. Thinking that one does not have an effect on the world, it was easy to retreat into the garden of their mind and let Rome decay. It should be no surprise that Stoicism flourished as the Roman Empire expanded and took away so much power and sovereignty that individual citizens formerly held.

These mollified men of modern America are not Stoics. There is no retreat into the mind or personal life. Men live a life filled with distractions now. It is the fear of change, the fear of disrupting the status quo, and the fear of the unknown. It is cowardice and fear, not praiseworthy endurance and resolve, which modern man exhibits. It is a dereliction of duty, not a virtuous outlook. Their dereliction does not have to be yours.

Someone will do something. An authority will take care of this. The law and the courts, maybe even the social media mob will grant you justice. In our feminized society, a consensus will be reached bestowing upon you some reward as the victim. These are all pleas. Everyone pleads to someone else for justice. The piece of paper may signal the system agreed, but you have to look in the mirror and believe it. When you assigned the power over to the authority to give you justice, you relinquished the right to declare something justice. It is their justice, not yours.

Someone will do something. This vibe permeates every nation. We see this around the world as our feminized international order sees challengers pop up who all fit a masculine mold. Whether in the Philippines, Italy, Hungary, Israel, Russia, America, or Brazil, there is a profile of the avatar for a masculine energy to restore order and deliver justice.

Sometimes, the joy is just in seeing one man say what people desperately want to say but feel they cannot. It is not even action, but mere words that exhilarate the supporters. These leaders are but men to sit atop grey bureaucracies that will fight them to keep our consensus, soft world in place. They cannot wield the sword or command forces to clean the Augean stables, yet people feel the threat is there just by their masculine pose. People want this masculine energy. These leaders become symbolic forms of it to fit their nations. They still do not change your home, your neighborhood, or your town. The street, the corner, and the path must be yours.

No one is coming to save you. You can assume the mantle of authority in your life. Build a life around you and it becomes your realm. A moment of crisis or confrontation may endanger you or a loved one. Do you have that spark to react and defend your honor and territory? Have you lived so that others know what stakes you are willing to risk for your honor and loved ones? In these times, confrontations can come from anywhere. There is no order, so chaos begets more chance for disputes.

If you live with fire openly, others will know and be inspired as well. This is not just for you to live, but for you to teach your children. Your moment of crisis will not be solitary if you live with this and carry that fire for others. If others have seen you stand up, they will fall into line. You will have support. Others will be there because of the example that you live. It may start with you, but that sovereignty and power will come back to the informal network of your community.

Deferring resolutions to third parties means that something has to be worth their time, whether their decision or you merely pleading for assistance. This becomes the grey zone that bad actors can pollute peaceful areas with their behavior. Your example stakes claim to that zone. Your example inspires others to act the same. The grey zone disappears. Order is formed even before our corrupt authorities are called to act. Your simple actions have created norms to instill order at the most base level.

CHAPTER 6

In any era, the man who develops his soul elevates himself to transcend our base materialism. This transcendence allows for greater understanding of his position in the world. In a chaotic world, this grounding makes him a boon to his community. Many wish to have everything broken down into small, understandable parts so they can claim to understand the whole. They do not see that this prevents them from the deeper understanding that there is a mystery to life. The only certainty in our world is uncertainty. In a superficial time, the man who develops his soul stands apart from the confused, hollow men around him. As your opponents in this spiritual war fire away at you, you must seek a means to fight back. No man can do it alone. One must know one's place in life and how one fits in. One must not just seek truth and wisdom, but seek the development of one's character and refinement of one's soul.

Your family, your line, has a religion. It was made by men to honor the gods that they thanked to put you there. If you reject it, you must light a candle and explain to those who came before why you reject what they built. If you follow it, you must sort yourself within the religion. You must engage in the rituals they set forth for the flock. You scoff at this. Maybe you call it a cargo cult mentality. But what did the great families in the fall of Rome or the Dark Ages do? They built, endured, and withstood the decline to make the future of Europe possible. The spiritual and religious is beyond the concept of immediate gratification.

As a member of this ADD-riddled culture, it is hard to escape this shallow mental framework and limited expectations. Is there a church or temple nearby? Enter and walk it again with new eyes. All around you, there are shrines, monasteries, and holy sites. This may surprise you because you live in a society that actively suppresses their existence while creating new shrines for people to worship. Seek out your people's sites. Look for the details left behind from those who came before and why. The details tell stories that mattered to them.

Listen to the words of the religious leaders. Do they reflect the eternal and time-tested beliefs, or are they recycled modern platitudes? Look beyond the immediate acts of contemporary men and dive into the eternal. There is a story in the architecture of the faith of those who built that site. The story was for them and for their posterity.

Do you honor your family's faith in your home? Start with one statue, one picture, or one small corner of a room. It will grow as your faith grows. As a child, you may have seen images, statues, and small relics of the faith in a grandparent's room or on a cabinet. This was their shrine to their faith and family. They took time, energy, and space from their innermost areas and quiet moments to honor their past. Why does no one do this now? This is mocked by others. Note of those others, do they honor their family and culture? Most criticism and derision is to make something low status. Those people do not honor their distant family, their religion, and their cultural traditions, so do you think they honor their families in the here and now? Walk a nursing home. If you consistently visit a relative there, you will wonder why no one else has steady visitors. Wonder no longer.

Forgetting to remember, honor, and celebrate ancestors, their faith, and their culture manifests later in a failure to celebrate and honor their living family. The person who does not celebrate or engage with their family does not understand their place in life. These are the people that are tossed in the chaos of our atomized society. With no grounding, they are swept in the winds of an ever-changing culture manipulated by entrenched mandarins.

The manipulative mandarins create a culture that encourages the mocking of old ways, faith and knowing one's history. Many may mock you for following the old ways, but if they are not going on the same journey, their words are meaningless. Examine those who do mock you. Physically examine them. Do they exhibit an appealing aesthetic? Examine them from a mental or emotional standpoint. Is their path leading to superior results?

Are they tossed in the winds of chaos? Have they secretly replaced the old religion with a new self-centered and consumer-friendly one? Many of these skeptics lack even the curiosity to develop their spirituality. The soul has not been relegated to a simple appendage or organ. Consider the widespread joke of selling one's soul as if it could be split from them and given away. Look at the physical atrophy of these skeptics and see also it in their souls. They have separated the soul from the mind, as if the mind could interpret the world around them without the soul.

For these incurious zombies, the soul simply does not exist. They have reduced the conception of the self to the pure materialist interpretation. Their minds point to a chemical and biological reason for everything. There is no transcendence in these lives chained to simply what can be proved, and not even by them, but by the priests of academia and their journalist scribes. They learn that they can rationalize any belief and activity to substitute for the holy and spiritual. They don't bother with robes or rituals. That would be too much effort. They just rationalize.

This makes their activities and beliefs even less rooted in reality than the rebellion of generations past. With ever-changing beliefs and practices, their minds are susceptible to the cultural whirlwind. Possibly they claim to be spiritual without being religious. This is cover. They know the emptiness of the atheist and want to avoid the stain of soullessness. Claiming to be above it all, they still worry what others think of their choice. What spirituality, then? The worship of the self.

Oh, but they traveled far, even sought a spiritual advisor. Did they tell you about it? Of course they did. Did they go on a vision quest at the right age, blessed by elders to walk the forests or wastelands? No. Did they go on a walkabout through the desert for weeks to test their mind and soul? No. Did they consume peyote and stare at the full moon in the desert night? No. Did they visit the holy sites in the desert or travel the forest roads to visit the old monasteries, temples, and churches of their faith? No. Did they beg for money and food outside temples and live only on that for months? No. They bought the experience. Just as any other discretionary purchase, it is consumed and disposed.

For $800, they visited a complex in a Peruvian jungle. They received mud baths, salt scrubs, and blessings from a three-foot tall Indio man. Selfies were taken. For $2,000, they visited a guru in India who recited platitudes about finding oneself and finding peace. Some even include relaxation days that have nothing to do with enlightenment, just comfort and exotic luxury. They did yoga, drank tea, and received rubdowns. Selfies were taken. They bought an experience. Not even an experience, but a marketed and carefully crafted facsimile of a true spiritual, religious experience. The latest practices, the pampering, and the exotic location were selected for the approval of their peers. It was not a lived experience, but a performance piece, neither spiritual nor religious. At the end of the spa week, they receive a blessing and certificate, but there was no power bestowed upon them.

They do not follow through with the lessons they learned, or follow through with a course of study on the religion's foundational myths. They may buy a candle or a picture as a souvenir of their spiritual awakening. The trip becomes a file they tuck away mentally to be pulled out and shown to others. Photographs were snapped for immediate sharing on social media, because all exotic spiritual retreats have Wi-Fi included. The pictures are tucked away in an online library, somewhere in a data center.

They learned a mantra. They tell you about it and even tell you their mantra. This is a token to wave as status over you who stands there without a mantra from the exotic, third world holy man. They forgot that to tell others your mantra is to destroy its power. Any spiritual aspect is erased by the manipulation of the experience into a commodity.

The further removed from their home culture, the more fake the experience. They can tell you about the holy man in the faraway land and yet be ignorant of their own people's local history. Their hometown may have been founded by religious zealots or other passionate idealists, but they don't care.

Severed from their past, they run to what the media system holds up as spiritual and good. They do not stop to think that the spirituality, peace, and power they seek can be found in the faith and art of their home culture. They never bothered to look. They would scoff at wearing a deer skull helmet from their home culture, but gleefully have Andean mud scraped from their legs to purify their spirit.

Skeptics look at the busts, statues, and cathedrals and move on. These don't speak to them because they don't reflect. Reflect on the hand that crafted an arch. A man designed it. Another man cut the stone for it. Another cut it to shape, and a team of men placed it into position. They did that for God, their church, and their fellow believers. Those churches took years or even centuries to complete. Many men worked knowing they would not see the final product, but they felt a part of something. It was not money that built those churches, but faith, drive, and community.

Now compare the soul of the contemporary naysayer staring at his phone, only pausing to lift it and spit out derision, to that of the man that laid a stone to build a church. He laid the stone knowing he would not live to see the church completed. He did not fear death, but welcomed the afterlife, where he could confidently say to his god that he honored and loved him.

The modern skeptic, arrogant in his atheism, is fearful of death. He does everything to avoid pain and the abyss of nothingness. He fears that this life is all he has, and he has done so little that he desperately clings to an extra year or more. The skeptic has no faith in an afterlife, though he may give you some vague quip on it. His skepticism of the eternal makes him seek the latest fad and the quickest purchase to alleviate this unease. He must feel good right now, lest he think of the nothing that awaits him. He wastes time and spirit rationalizing his decisions, down to the simplest of social urges, to give each thing meaning and affirm his worldview.

The skeptic will not humble himself before a god, and he will not honor the chorus of ancestors who filled the churches for ages. But they sing to you. Honor them. Honor their sacrifice. Pray as they did. Do not pray for trinkets and baubles. Pray to have the wisdom and power to accomplish your goals.

There is a saint associated with your name. There are heroes for your sect, tribe, and country. Who are they and what did they do for your people? The heroes of old and those who honored them wished to see those traits exhibited in you. These stories of struggle, perseverance, and renewal are eternal. Some heroes had to claim a home in a foreign land and protect their families from hostile forces. This is your task in these times of chaos. There are troubles in your land, and forces can enter your home via many channels. Seek the old rituals. Seek these figures. Pray.

The man who prays humbles himself. He knows that there are elements beyond his control and influence. There is the sphere of control and sphere of influence, and outside of that the gods tend. The man who prays can silence the world for minutes. The man who can meditate for five minutes is a man apart. This is an expression of willpower and reclamation of sovereignty.

Even the simplest meditation, like focusing on one's breathing, can bring about changes in your mental state. Directing the focus of the meditation can bring you to a better understanding of your body and purpose. How many of your friends and family members cannot sit still for a few minutes before lunging at their phone? These troubled, anxious souls cannot go it alone. Light a candle and pray for them.

In their anxiety, they relinquish their minds to the world out there and not the immediate. The location of one's attention is the location of one's mind. They are not present. The man who can meditate will feel less stress and will develop powers of concentration. He can focus on the present and be mindful of his surroundings. This man can set himself in order. With knowledge of his immediate surroundings, he can lead and bring order to his circle.

A man who understands where he fits into his chain of history and the web of today can judge and act. When an understanding of place is combined with a mind that studies, a man can be thought of as a leader due to his strong *phronesis*. *Phronesis* is another ancient Greek virtue that men can come to exemplify for their community. It is the idea of prudence, practical wisdom, and mindfulness. It is not merely disembodied thought, unaware of your presence and role, but intelligence with a moral and ethical foundation, wisdom. *Phronesis* is the virtue of the leader of sound judgment. It is the wisdom of a man fully integrated in his world.

This is an interconnected, specialized world, therefore no man can do this alone. A man with *phronesis* can judge and find other good men, who together will be trusted by their community to act in accordance with truth. They can find the humility to follow their ancestors and the knowledge to carry their community forward.

CHAPTER 7

Art must be a part of one's life.

Ignore the filthy works trumpeted as art by our cultural mandarins. That is art that reflects our chaos and decay. It is art for a junk society. It is not for you. You seek truth and beauty. Are you an artist? Do you have talent? Even if long since practiced, bring back your talents. Practice again. Even an amateur can produce works that bring light to friends and family.

Art is the expression of the human condition. It is a celebration or rebellion of the spirit. It expresses the triumph and struggle of the soul. Those paintings from centuries ago portray your forefathers, their exploits, hopes, and fears. To know this is to recognize that the twisted art of today reflects a society that yells about everything but that which matters. Some paint in bodily fluids in order to shock, but so many now do that that it simply bores and repulses. This is art of a demotic age where anyone can create, and many believe they should. They do not seek to place themselves under masters, but shout their message into the void and demand recognition. This is another symptom of contemporary man's vanity. Few humble themselves to God. Even fewer humble themselves before a fellow man. With amateur skills, they demand praise.

There is beautiful art out there. Seek it, appreciate it, and find its meaning. Encourage the artists. Art is not just produced. Creation is only part of the story. There is also the patronage, promotion, and transmission by those who recognize and enjoy it. It is their duty, as well as artists', to make understood the lessons in art and what they signify for society. If art does not speak to people of the artist's own culture, then the art is separated from its culture. The artist is disconnected. The chain of cultural transmission has been severed.

As indoctrinated and confused as we are in this age of chaos, we still recoil from modern art. The culture that we come from echoes in our souls and is expressed in this revulsion. We remember. Few can express it properly, and others are afraid the mandarins will call them foolish, but we still know the difference between beauty and ugliness, form and chaos.

If you can create, create. If you cannot, celebrate what is beautiful. Include others. Art connects, as the mind completes the art through the act of witnessing. What have others seen that you missed? Be humble and open to their interpretations. There are artists in your community. Find them. Help them. You can become a patron. You select the artist. You guide the art made. It becomes a shared story.

Do local schools have arts programs? Contact those educators. You can provide a scholarship. You can provide supplies and fund programs. Artists in days of yore had patrons they knew. Artists of today plead for money from a faceless, bureaucratic government. These artists producing forgettable art applied for grants via a website. They learned at schools that spoke of many qualities before ever discussing truth or beauty. They are part of a culture that has forgotten about truth and beauty, fled from them, lied about them, pretended they are subjective. They treat them as subjective and smear the very ideas because they are afraid they will never create anything true or beautiful. They fear failure.

The trappings of the artist are what drew them to the art world. They did not have the spark to create. It was a role that they assumed. That role has been molded by cultural authorities, and anyone willing to assume the identity and spout the right lines will do. These artists are not people born with the need to create. They have forgotten the *why* behind art, which is why their art is forgettable. It is why they push filth. It is at their level. It reflects their emptiness. They just wanted the lifestyle of the artist so the product does not matter.

One art show hosted a variety of artists and potential donors. A walkthrough for the visual artists was followed by a dance troupe's piece and then cocktails for mingling. The various artist types were on display. The glasses, the hair, the clothes, even the sexualities. Everything was selected to present the artist for the donor to see, like, and award with his or her patronage.

Minutes into the cocktail session, the doors opened and a tall, very skinny man entered. He wore sunglasses in the evening, tight jeans, biker boots, a dirty T-shirt, and a jean jacket with patches. He paused and allowed three others to flank him. To his right was a shorter fat man all in black, sunglasses, and a beard. To his left was a thin brunette in sunglasses and a black short dress. She wore her hair in a bun and had legs and an hourglass figure that would excite any man. To her left was a short, petite blonde, also in sunglasses and a short black dress.

After they assembled, the posse marched. The artist's bulky boots snapped a beat. It was a confident walk. People turned to look at them. The crowd of 100 was captivated. All small talk stopped. This was a man that commanded attention. It was impressive. But the event photographer intervened. This older gentleman stopped them after 20 supremely confident strides and asked if they could go back and re-enter so he could get another take.

What did *the artist* do? A true artist would have kept walking. He would have dismissed the photographer. This was his moment. His time to announce to the enchanted audience that he had arrived, time to proudly explain his work and impress donors. What explanation was needed? He would not need to explain, for it would be as powerful as his entrance. The donors would rain money on him just to be associated with such an artist. He did not do this. He stopped his crew, and they returned to the entrance to walk again.

The comedy of errors began as the photographer could not get the shot he wanted. They walked the hallway four times. Lighting was off. The pace was not in sync this time. Ah, another angle! The crowd lost patience and its attention faded. This artist was not born or made an artist through years of apprenticeship. He had chosen to live the lifestyle and had received the appropriate credentials. The hairstyle, scruffy beard, and clothing were the final pieces of a costume to finish the act.

A curious observer would have tracked down the art created by the man with the grand entrance. It was photography of an Industrial Punk aesthetic. The brunette was a model for him. She had a welder's mask on, drills in hand, and posed in photos among the mid-20th century industrial ruins. She wore jean shorts and a torn-up white tank top, and her body was striped with paint and strategically smeared with grease. The artist's display was just sex wrapped in Detroit Decline packaging. More men paid attention to the brunette than the artist's work for the rest of the soiree.

Standing by his work, other artists approached him, but over the course of the hour, he had few donors approach. He had revealed the fraud of the entire night. The patrons were looking for an artist that was the artist type, but they did not want it rubbed in their faces that it was all an act. These are not artists, and the donors are just checkbook patrons. Nothing is really created to last beyond the transaction and the later reference to the transactional relationship. Nothing will be truly remembered.

Seek out memorable art. Take in the classics, train your eye, and be open to discovering talent and promise among our contemporaries. If you have talent, create; if not, sponsor worthy artists or simply share in humanity's striving for beauty. Not just to remember, but to renew the spirit. You feed your mind and body to fuel the fire of the soul. Art is but accelerant for that flame.

CHAPTER 8

Not all men are suited for the fine arts, but any man can work with his hands and mind for the betterment of his home and community. The Greeks valued *techne,* what we call the mechanical arts or trades. This is an area in which all men should accumulate skills.

Our very names reveal familial history in the trades. Explore your own lines and look for the stories behind the names. A surname related to a trade is how your ancestors were identified. Can you fulfill an old role? The contemporary man places himself above his ancestors, yet cannot perform the basic functions these dead men found second nature. How many contemporary men reach for their phone the moment something breaks? It is not just not knowing how to do handiwork, but not even exhibiting the curiosity to learn small skills. Contemporary men can hang a picture. The rest they outsource.

This is the core of modern man's problems. He has outsourced everything but the most basic, immediate functions. The modern man can never leave his room if he wants. The Japanese suffer this growing problem and call these adults *hikikomori.* There is someone else available to do anything he needs. This has pervades every aspect of a man's life. He has forgotten what he is capable of on his own.

He will not install a cabinet. A contractor will do it. He will not teach his child about sex. The schools will do it. He will not befriend his neighbors to better police his neighborhood. The city will do that. He will not guide his daughter's relationships or protect her. Magazines and restraining orders will do that.

Modern men are programmed to avoid such tasks because broader society does not value them in such roles. The tasks themselves mean responsibility, duty, and if they fail, blame. Your grandfather had a wall of specialized tools for a myriad of applications. Your father had a toolbox in the garage for emergencies. You have a hammer and two screwdrivers in a drawer. Maybe your father was absent or failed to explain the hows and whats behind quick fixes. Maybe they didn't want you to have to do them.

Many a blue-collar father's dream is that his son never has to sweat or break his back on the job. His son can avoid the daily grind he endured. It was a well-intentioned hope for an easier future. What those fathers did not imagine was that their sons would lose all of those skills that generations of fathers found perfunctory. Those fathers did not imagine their sons would find emptiness and no sense of accomplishment in their comfortable, air-conditioned offices. There is no satisfaction in ten percent close ratios, contract evaluations, or supply chain management that compares to a newly-painted home, an assembled engine, or a finished cabinet.

As a first step to reclaiming this part of your birthright, tackle small tasks and learn basic skills that were once considered second nature. Once a trade is learned or a new skill is developed and refined, it can never be taken from a man. Possessions, money, and even friends come and go, but what a man can do with his mind and hands he will always have.

Start small with basic tools and household fixes, and build to greater jobs. Begin with the hand tools: a saw, a hammer, a chisel, sandpaper. You might have had an uncle or a grandfather that showed you his trade or the craft that he was passionate about. He showed you for a reason. The finished products were why you stood his workshop, smelling the sawdust, wearing safety glasses too big for your head. The craftsman needed to share how it came to be and how you fit into it all. In sharing his passion, he was hoping you would pick it up as well. That it would live on in you.

There was a small project you could do together. He may have even let you pick it out. A shelf for your mother on Mother's Day. A box for storing action figures. A short bookcase because you were finally reading on your own. This man had seen you grow up and realized you were old enough to learn and value learning. Your mind and body were old enough to follow instructions and properly handle a saw, sander, or drill.

Rather than use the new saws and machinery, he might have grabbed the old tools that he learned with or had assembled over years of work. There were differences between using a disc sander, sanding by hand, using rough sandpaper, or finishing paper. A craftsman knows these things. He was going to show you how the tool and the craftsman come together to give the work meaning. Using a bench plane may not have been as fast as a machine, but it was a skill to develop to feel the wood. The silky finish to a piece of wood after you have worked it would be more satisfying than running it through a machine.

Undoubtedly, introducing you to his workspace, you were going to slow down his project. He'd give you a piece of wood and some tools to chip and carve. This was to get you out of his way, but also to allow you to try on your own. It was an invitation to his creative laboratory. He shared the experience with you.

Your hands, arms, and mind would develop a feel for the effort involved to get the right finish. Under his effort, your skills would develop slowly. The craftsman carved a new craftsman. The older men trained their replacements, the family's new artisans, with the promise that maybe they would elevate the skills and accomplishments of the line.

A man who can build and shape is always valued. Whether an A-frame cabin or a simple shelf, there is value in creation. The recipient is always connected to the creator. This is a disposable society with an abundance of manufactured objects. To bestow a gift that is handmade has a different connotation than just a generation ago. Handmade had a different status when manufactured goods were a premium. Whether the widespread loss of skill, or the appreciation for the time, energy, and effort that goes into a handmade gift, these gifts assume more meaning now.

In the chaos of our society, many people hit low points and have nothing. Reaching out with a simple creation and sharing your skill can help them reconnect. If not with the broader community, they connect with one person. Once they learn a skill, they can connect to that community and fellow craftsmen. If ten, twenty, or thirty years ago someone valued showing you how, what and why one learned a craft, it is worth it to start anew.

The raw material waits for the tradesman's hand and the craftsman's thoughts. It is up to you to pick it up and create. It is up to you to teach the next generation.

CHAPTER 9

Aim to become a leader, a man worthy of emulation. This will happen by degrees as you study, train, and do. You want to lead by example, and through charisma, the state of grace that comes to those in command of themselves.

A man has emotions, but a strong man understands his emotions and is not controlled by them. Which man leaves a lasting effect: the man who is agitated with every slight, or the man who rages at the appropriate moment? The man who rages at everything places no qualm, argument, or misfortune in context. He creates confusion and anxiety, and others will avoid him. Such a man is no leader, and if he is nominally in such a position, his only way to motivate will be through fear.

When voices from media outlets discuss men, feelings, and being more emotional, what do they seek? Pride, anger, and determination are all emotions that men exhibit every day. These are not the feelings and emotions the media frames as men opening up and being emotional. Our authorities want men to show vulnerability, express confusion, or play the victim. This is what being emotional means for the managed chaos that is contemporary society.

In the realm of love, there is a difference between the man who falls hard for a woman and the man who chases love, giving his own at the slightest return. Both love. Both can be passionate. One is a man who is himself and has found a person with whom he can transcend the mundane. The other is a man who has crafted a persona to emulate some contrived role.

As you develop your mind, body, and soul and integrate yourself into your community, women will gravitate towards you. Others will direct women your way. The man who sorts out his place in society can sort out his emotions. He will understand and harness them.

Look at the nominal adults who proclaim to be blind with rage, trembling with anger, shaking with fear, or triggered by mere words or simple images. They are children. They have no control over themselves. Worse, they are liars. They affect outrage, not realizing it reflects a childish relationship with their emotions. The man who masters his emotions understands his real needs. He will not be persuaded and lied to by mass marketing tested in laboratories. His interests are the eternal. His orientation is focused on cultivating himself and his immediate circle.

This is not to say man is a static entity and emotionless. Man is portrayed in contemporary media as someone things happen to. You want to be a dynamic force that sets things in motion. Do not bottle and suppress, because we all know the man who buries his feelings, whether justified reactions or spurious rushes. That man will stuff every flicker of emotion.

Consider the flow of emotions like a river that empties into the ocean. It is not all pure, clear water, but carries silt and mud that can block a channel if not dredged. A man could internalize and never face his emotions. He will puddle up, spread out, go stagnant. Then one day, he breaches his banks and pours out a destructive rage. The tiniest annoyance will set him off cursing at a dear friend or family member. He will hurt or destroy something simply because he did not harness his emotions earlier. This is the man that tolerates nagging and slights from his wife, minor insults from others, and slogs through a brutal job. We know he tolerates it until the day when he has had enough. He does more damage in his final release than he would have in steady management of those nuisances. He endured and let it slide because he wanted to be nice. He did not want to upset anybody. He did not want to lead.

Strong men are often described as rocks, but do not let that become the one defining feature, robustness. Life is not merely enduring. A leader is not just strong like a rock, but is persistent like the waves on the shore. The waves can wear down the rock to nothing. A man armed with the truth is like the waves, for he is always there and will always win.

A man must harness his emotions and not just be running for

approval from one person to the next or running for love from one woman to the next. A man who sorts himself out, harnesses truth, and develops his character becomes the man who may fall hard for a good woman but not the man who chases love.

To love deeply is one of life's gifts, but to hate is also part of life. A man cannot properly understand humanity or himself until he has both loved and hated deeply. To have truly loved is to know there is something you'd sacrifice your life for, and to truly hate is to know there is something you would destroy.

A leader needs to have experienced and processed many emotions. It is their judicious expression that distinguishes him from the masses, that allows him to find his purpose not merely through contemplation, which is prone to stray from reality, but through his experience contending with this world.

CHAPTER 10

Two men sit together at a birthday party. Both are 40. One has a wife and children. The other has neither. The oldest child walks up to his father and hugs him before running off to play. The bachelor says to the father, "I so want what you have." The family man replies, "I am lucky." They move on in their conversation.

Both of these men miss the reality of the situation. Both men failed in some regard. These small failures are why men are in this mess. The bachelor said he wanted what the family man had. He did not ask him how he did it. He did not seek advice. He simply wanted. Without any discussion, he could not be sure that he wanted it. The bachelor would not defer to the family man and be taught. He would not admit a failing and an area for improvement.

There is a possibility that family life would make him recoil if he understood the responsibilities it entailed. The family man enjoys the fruit of hard work, but it is not always a joy. It comes with duties and responsibilities. The father and husband that puts in no effort is steamrolled by his wife and mocked by his kids. That is bitter fruit and the diet of some family men.

Our culture is obsessed with the individual. This prevents people from entering into even a situationally subordinate position, where one is no longer an individual but part of a whole. Subordinate is not always inferior. One may submit provisionally to a skilled teacher with no loss of wider status. The subordinate seeks the means to become a master. There is nothing inferior in that act. Awash in egalitarian messaging, modern man cannot bear to voluntarily submit as an inferior. Without deferring to the experience of others, how does an individual even know how to begin?

The family man above shirked his responsibility to his fellow man. He told a partial truth when he claimed to be lucky. He did not explain how he formed his family. He did not even correct or affirm the bachelor's appraisal. Being the same age, the family man could ask what the bachelor had done for the last 20 years. If this was a slow realization via years of observation, the family man could explain how to actively walk his path, but he did not want to fulfill the role of teacher. He feared the responsibility. Maybe nobody had instructed him either, so how could he deign to advise another? Besides, he is told by the media that a father is just a paycheck, that a man is to a woman as a bicycle is to a fish.

No man should be passive in this life. Whether carving roads out of mountains or molding the souls of the next generation, creation and craftsmanship need active men. Starting a family is like any task. It needs to have a plan. A partner cannot just be anyone, but someone committed to the project with the same vigor. A family needs a man to put the plan into motion. Not all men are so suited. Some are meant to be passionate creators or crusaders.

Once a man has entered the bonds of matrimony, he becomes a leader, and a greater leader still as a father. The freedom of the solitary man is surrendered for the duty of being the steward of the future. The man who takes the first step toward marriage must transform into a new being. It is a role he consciously or unconsciously saw in his future. The 40-year-old man smiling at his wife holding his child was a man at 22 who took steps to be in that position at 40.

"*But women are fat,*" complains a bachelor. There is no denying the porcine appearance of many contemporary women. This man does not think to elevate his wealth and physique to be admitted to better pools of women.

"*But women are wicked,*" the young shout. Women have always been wicked. The wicked prey on the weak. Do not be weak.

"*But they are all feminists,*" the college men yell. How many girls have assumed those beliefs like they do annual fashions? Offer an alternative, be strong, and the right woman will follow.

"*But they are harpies and ball-busters,*" men in bars complain. She tests your fortitude. Agree and amplify. Laugh it off. Make her feel lucky to be in your life, not the other way around.

"But women are skanks," the young men cry. Read tales from decades and centuries ago. This type has always existed. Where are you meeting women? Select a different pool for the future mother of your children. If she can't cook, there is no reason for her to stay at your place after sex. Why should she enjoy a safe night under the roof you provide?

Expect more, demand more. Women will treat you the way you allow. What are you looking for? The needs for a lifetime are different than the desires for one night. Who told you what type of woman to look for? Was it the same media that denigrates your place in society? Do not listen to them. Read the surveys of what men say they want in a wife. Compare them to the surveys of 50 years or a century ago. What did they look for now versus then? Which era had marital security and which era had marital chaos?

The media wants you to want a physically strong, snarky, ambitious woman. This is the same media that portrays men as out of touch buffoons or malicious monsters. Newer surveys show the desire to be a mother as low on a list for prospective wife qualities. How has modern man been conditioned to enter permanent bonds with women with no hint at children? Man has long entered marriage to bring children forth, not to joke about television shows with witty, crude jokes for 40 years. Clear your mind of such notions, and follow your instincts, for they are honest and guided by evolution.

Don't be a sap, but be honest about yourself, too. The woman you trick with words will be crushed when your reality is revealed. This is the man she will speak of to your child. You should be a man who doesn't need to hide behind words.

If it is for the carnal delights of the night, then pull in the hottest body you can find, but be careful. Once you have a child, your will is no longer entirely yours. And be careful not to become a trained clown, repeating the same moves to amuse a parade of low-value women.

If you claim to want a family, then you must seek a woman who wants a family. She may not say so at 22, but does she have the signs of a future mother? Place a baby in her arms. The more she looks at it and the less she looks at you holding the baby, the better. Watch her around children. Watch her around her grandparents. Watch her behavior when a friend is ill. Watch her with her dog. If a woman can dress up a dog and cry at its vet visits, she will cry for a child and already wants one, even if she doesn't know it yet. She just has not found a man to lead her to motherhood, one who satisfied her primal standards. Many women have confessed, "I would not have another one of his children." Sometimes that sentiment develops before the first has arrived.

You mold yourself into a man of iron to attract worthy women. Don't waste your time with the unworthy. It is better to be single, refining your talents, than to waste a second with the unworthy. Each improvement, each new talent, and every dollar you earn opens doors to better women.

So many women lack the basic skills of their ancestors, and can offer only the siren song of sex. Modern men esteem what is in effect masturbating into a woman, even one resembling a circus sideshow fat lady. *"What a loser, he is well-rounded and does not sleep with women. I am cooler. I'm sleeping with this walrus."* The media laughs at masculine pursuits except one: sex with women. They want you chasing women to feel like a man. It is the only approved venue in which men can compete against one another, one in which women are the arbiters. Consider the reflexive insult of any political opponent: "sex deprived." Consider the reflexive insult from any woman: "poor cocksmanship." They approve of blobs who wear children's clothing and barely live adult lives, but the immediate insult is to sexual prowess. They know that is how you have chosen to define your worth. Deny them this. You seek the approval of greater figures, the men of the ages. Sexual prowess is to be esteemed, but to be led by your genitals is to be a teenager. The men from your line would be impressed by your bedding dozens of women. They would expect conquered villages and monuments left to your glory. But unless your notch count is the side-effect of such a life, they would be puzzled or even disgusted. Deny unworthy women your essence and you will think clearer around the worthy.

You have sought teachers for study, for fitness, and for life. Do not be ashamed to seek help with finding a worthy woman. There are many men online who discuss the latest tools and methods to find and seduce women. When seeking a woman who could be the mother of your children, help is there if you are willing to reach out for it. Close observers of your life may know more worthy matches for you than you can find in a bar or at a party.

Disregard what women say they want in men. They are saying it for their immediate audience, to appear a woman of the zeitgeist. Women revealed their true selves when they devoured *50 Shades of Grey*. Many will push it further than the clearly sanitized acts portrayed in the book. What do women want? A handsome, fit man of money and mystery who can make them scream. What do they want? A leader and a monster who will let her into his life. The air of dark mystery is the feeling you give them when they are unsure of how you see them but you are absolutely sure of yourself.

The man who brings flowers to his woman every week walks into a trap of his own making. The week that he forgets will be the one she never will. The man who never gets his woman flowers leaves open a powerful possibility. The week that he does will be the one she will always remember. There is no sense in being a harmless rabbit, even if it is your nature. She wants a mysterious or dangerous animal who can show clemency and make an exception for her benefit.

Women want a leader, a man that is his own and makes her a part of his life. Consider the couples where the woman keeps her own name in marriage, and how that increases their odds of divorce. One house, one name. If you are relinquishing your freedom to build a family with her, she should gladly take your name. The sharp-tongued woman who claims to belong to no man would purr like a kitten for one she found worthy. Don't believe the excuses women come up with to cover for their noncommittal behavior. Maybe she says it's for her career, as if she is destined for the corner office and executive salary. Forget the millions of successful married women for whom a name change was no hindrance (also forget that nobody really cares how much money a woman makes).

To these independent women, you just play a supporting role. To surrender your freedom sacrifices plenty of pursuits you, a free man, could follow. She should sacrifice her father's name to the tribe you are building together. Rejecting your name shows a reluctance to join your tribe, a refusal to acknowledge your leadership. No woman questions taking the name of a man that she respects. If you were to have children, how would you explain it to them? If their mother does not share your name, then what else about your family might they reject?

CHAPTER 11

With a woman walking through life with you, a child will follow. You are not the first nor last person to have a child. You will not be the best or the worst parent. You will make mistakes. There will be moments of good fortune. Allow others to hold and enjoy your child while an infant. The baby will survive and you can enjoy the rest. Avoid playing the martyr. Your ancestors raised children with far less than what you have and in far worse circumstances.

A baby has few needs. The mother can provide all of those. Very soon, however, the needs grow. The little soul begins to show. This soul will need molding and guidance. You must consider your duty and lead, not just for your child, but for the men who have came before you. Did they shirk their duties as role models? Maybe your father did, but you can make it right and restart the chain. In his failure, you learned what matters more than the pick-ups and errands of fatherhood. You are your child's first model of a man. A boy will emulate your behavior, and all her life a girl will seek men like you or run from them.

Include extended family as much as possible in your child's life. Their personalities will develop more fully if you give them a variety of figures to interact with. Children are always watching. They watch as we talk and move and extrapolate what we are thinking. They copy strength. They copy what is pleasing and beautiful. They will think as you do, so think virtuous thoughts. A child that sees his father humble himself before God will learn that humbling himself before his parents is natural.

Think of your studies, your physical activity, and prayer. If children see this, they will emulate it, and it will come naturally all their lives. A child does not navigate a maze on his first attempt. He does not build a tall tower of blocks on the first try. A child must practice with easy tasks and work his way up. Lead. Even if a child cannot help you with a task or understand your rituals, it is good to include them as a passive observer. The child that sits beside you while you read and holds a book upside down is more likely to become a reader himself.

Roughhouse, wrestle, and be active with your children, for age catches up with you fast. Exposure to vigorous play will keep them active even when you are not around. Play-fighting also exposes your kids to physical activity separate from actual anger and punishment. They will not run from any conflict simply because of the presentation of force. They will learn context. There will come a moment where they will hit you. It will hurt. They will realize their growing power. To be a man is to be aware of the possibility of physical violence. To sanitize one's persona of all aggressive tendencies is to abdicate a responsibility. Look at children's entertainment today. Why do all the male figures seem gay? They aren't, but they act feminine. They have been stripped of any sense of violence, any capability to attack or protect. These are cardboard cutouts, neutered men.

Develop small traditions that are open to other family members and friends. Hiking can become something not just shared between you and your child, but with others. This becomes family tradition. Allow children to have traditions with uncles, aunts, and cousins, for small joys in their life can come from unexpected relationships. The person they may turn to in a crisis might be one of them and not you.

Not every misdeed is to be met with a storm. A child need not learn that every misstep is the chance for anger and punishment. They must not fear an accident. They must not be afraid to act. Pay attention to children that seek to assign blame for mere accidents. They reveal a child that is fearful of established punishments.

A child must learn that you are a fair judge, for if they don't trust you, they will hide misdeeds. Consider it positive that they come asking for forgiveness rather than hide from parental judgment.

Children must learn to follow through and complete tasks. Start young. Take the time to develop their determination and the positive feelings that come with achievement. Tasks left undone and half-completed build up to a life that is half-lived.

There is much moaning about the death of family dinnertime. Why? Why, in a nation that watches six hours of television a night, is there not an hour for meal preparation and dining? It is not a priority. A meal allows for discussion of the day. Think of the things you can learn about your children's lives and they learn about you in that setting. Not just this exchange of information and sharing of lives, but your children learn to act appropriately with adults. A child who can eat with his parents without fuss can eat in public. This is part of a child's training to be a member of society.

Children are naturally curious. This world is new to them. Encourage this trait as a way to develop a curious intellect. Do not be short with the child that asks questions. Use humor to end a line of questioning when a child turns into a prosecutor. Children are always surprised, and their minds lose focus when an adult drops to their level. Children will ask you many questions, progressing from what to how to why. As a child is continuously learning, you too will have to stay continuously learning.

Did your parents complain that their parents did not understand? Did you wonder why your parents let you get away with so much? Did you laugh at how you ran circles around them with technology and access to its temptations? What did those failures create? Learn from their missteps or you will be another out-of-touch parent.

The mind is where the attention is. The days where you have your child's full attention and trust are limited. As the leader of the household, you filter the world and its meaning for them. You allow them to interact with it on their own where you deem it appropriate. If they go to schools, they have a circle of children that tell them about the world. Do you know your children's friends' names? Do you know their parents? This should be the least of things you know about them. If they watch television, someone else is telling them about the world. Do you know the plots of the shows your children watch? Why even allow it? If you allow it, be engaged and control what is watched.

There is a box. It has access to all of the world's temptations, evils, and filth. Anything the mind can conjure up and things unimaginable are shown on this box. It will never stop sending images. It will recommend more as if it knows you the more you use it. It will not just try to read your mind but nudge it along paths for its gain.

Why would anyone let this box into their home? Why would anyone let a child play with this box? Who would pay for such a box? But almost every home has a computer. Left unattended, the box is a gateway to anything your child can think up. Carefully craft the need for this in your home. If you need it, carefully structure access to it. Others face this predicament and have the same concerns. The computer is a tool. The Internet is a tool. Use of the tool depends on the hand that wields it. These wonderful tools can be manipulated for others to make money and corrupt souls. The seven deadly sins never went away, they just found new hiding spots.

No matter your efforts, children will emulate and rebel. It is natural as they age and attempt to carve out their identity. You must still lead. You are not their friend but their father. You lead towards the path of adulthood.

Did the parents that indulged in fads see superior results? A parent being a friend and a cool parent has surrendered authority in serious situations, not just the fun times. What defines a cool parent? Was it listening to the Beatles and allowing a beer in '68? Was it allowing pot smoking and parties that mom and dad supervised in '92? Was it introducing your daughter to heroin in '10? Cool is ephemeral and forever changing so that it can be marketed as new to spice up life. A cool parent is a media-concocted meme.

Even before the middle-aged parent can sadly pretend to be cool, there are the young parents that use the softest voice possible to politely ask a three-year-old to make a decision. One stands there listening to their tone oscillating between pleading and condescending. The annoyance you feel rising in your chest is a revulsion at the parent's weakness. The child is a child that barely understands anything. Make a decision and move on with life.

If the soft, condescending parent angers you the adult, imagine how their teenage children full of hormones and adult ideas will view them. With a parent as a friend and not a father, the child does not see the natural progression to adulthood. The authority of one's role as parent is undermined by the friend status. Parent, even adult, becomes a role they vaguely understand. Adults roaming Disney World with coloring books but no children in tow never learned the clear demarcation of child and adult. They saw someone supposedly in the role deny they were that role.

If children do not see a parent fulfilling that traditional role, what faith will they have in anyone? This is a simple, daily expression of hierarchy, duties, and responsibilities both up and down the ladder.

There may come a point where your child will surpass you. Physically, mentally, emotionally, or in their achievements. This is a glorious thing. This is your lasting legacy on this mortal earth. The insecure parent will consider this a threat to their status, not a reflection of the child and all that the parent did to guide them. A secure parent will recognize that a gifted child is a blessing. There are accomplishments and tasks that they can tackle that you never could have or might never have thought worthy of approaching. You have poured your essence into them. They are part of you in both the material and mystical sense. This is your work.

There will come a time where your children will change from people you live with to people who visit you. Being a parent is the job that never ends. You only change the function of your role. The majesty of the authority figure will fade with time, and the child will create a three-dimensional conception of you. When they have looked beyond the mere status of father, what type of man will they see? This remains and dominates well after they have left your home. The role lasts until you die. Not the active duty, but the mental and emotional attachment. Learn to develop and age into new roles as your children age. The engaged, active father can mature into the consulting guru or elder statesman who has seen it all.

The timing of your death does not matter. Your example should be lived at all stages in life to last for all ages. It goes beyond death. Did you live as a man that your children will fondly recall? Did you start traditions or restart old ones to pass down? You can become the ideal for not just one generation, but many.

CHAPTER 12

There are languishing traditions that you could share with your children, but you would have to start them alone. Some of these are tied to the very start of the formation of the masculine role. One such tradition is hunting. The hunt now is not for sustenance and survival, but is a choice by the vast majority that practice. This was not always the case, and game itself was always going to be limited in frequency and number. It would be a privilege to hunt, and an earned place to be considered a valuable hunter.

There are some men with minds so weakened that they openly admit fear of holding a weapon. They don't feel the laughter of their ancestors, who all kept swords, spears, knives, and rifles in their homes when allowed, and sometimes when not. Transfer the fearful man's statements or arguments against owning a gun or rifle to medieval days. Think of how ridiculous it would sound to say no one needed a gladius in their home. The fabled medieval authorities, corruption and all, would protect them in a snap. Imagine the argument for purely defensive weapons, *"What does one need a sword for? One could accidentally die from mishandling one in their villa! Did you know thousands of Franks kill themselves with a sword each year? A shield can protect you and not incidentally kill anyone. Only the king's men should have swords."*

The aversion to guns lies in the political belief system that enslaves the thought process and requires signaling compliance at every possible moment. Hunting requires familiarity and practice handling a weapon. It is a tool. A simple session at a gun range or a makeshift target in the woods would demystify the objects so demonized by the cultural gatekeepers.

To hunt is also to push back on societal programming that considers it

71

low status and makes it a source of derision. Hunting is considered a hick activity that the rubes engage in across flyover country. Disney has spent decades mocking it for children to see. This is not just in the antagonist of cute animal pictures, but in shorts that portrayed hunters as beer-swilling hayseeds that shot at anything that moved. Listen to the wine-sipping man's criticism, *"It's so easy with a rifle."* They then turn their head for the next three-minute political point. Those are the words of a person who has never woken up at 3AM to get dressed. They have never quietly walked trails in the woods, looking for signs and smelling for scents. They have never masked their own scent and been still for five minutes, let alone the hours of a hunt. They have never selected a spot to patiently wait or use a well-practiced call. They have never stalked anything that moved as fast as a car and spooked at the slightest sound.

Easy is the word used by a man who never saw a beast and felt the rush in their body that this was their chance for the season. Had to carefully raise their rifle for their one shot. They have not done it and cannot do it, therefore they smear it as beneath them or barbaric. These practices of their ancestors and even the men that they may have known as children are to be mocked. It cannot simply be allowed to be. If not smeared with a negative label, others may elevate it above what they do.

The ancients would often send boys into the forest as a test. This challenge was a journey out of the comfort of the community. It was not just out of material comfort and security, but the cultural rules and mores that bound him. In the forest, he learned about nature, about power, and about his true self. The laws of nature sometimes collided with what he had been told as a child in the village. When he returned, he was a man. He had engaged with the wild, it had changed him and he returned a survivor.

Many of those that mock hunting fail to see the challenge of simply setting foot on one's own into the woods. They fail to see the ritual that is being repeated. How many have walked alone in the woods? Walking along a carefully cleared trail with signs labeling the streams and importance of the watershed, the valley, or certain tree species does not count. There is no challenge or danger there. Once again, the contemporary man has substituted a pre-packaged consumer experience for a natural, older ritual.

This has destroyed the meaning of climbing Mount Everest. Once the impossible summit, it was climbed by heroic men seeking to conquer nature. Look at the summit now and it looks like a velvet rope-corralled line at a nightclub in snow. Spending good money, these new men and women simply want the photo and the marketed trip. It is devoid of soul. It is no accomplishment. It is a purchase.

The weekend spent on the hunt for a wild animal for the potential to enjoy meals won with hard work is a crude fall pastime. In their eyes, eating processed food and watching steroided up semi-literates collide with one another is superior. *"It is barbaric,"* they text you from their device made with materials collected by African child labor in mines while wearing shoes made in Asian sweatshops.

It is different. That is all. The man from a century earlier would recognize the hunter of today walking in the woods, albeit in slightly different garb, more than he would the couch potato in front of a 60-inch HDTV. To hunt is to engage in a long tradition and to become aware of one's environment.

Hunting is not the cartoonish hyperbole that resides in mass media depictions. It is a means to connect with the wild portions of our domains and to recognize their importance.

Hunting opens the way to true environmentalism. One must spend time in the environment. Trudging through snow and on the hunt is not in the current public conception of environmentalism, but what is checking "like" for green awareness social media pages? Environmentalism doesn't mean checking off academically-approved good deeds. It means understanding both man's insignificance in the universe and our role as stewards of the earth.

Once one is aware of the needs of the forest wildlife, conservation naturally follows. It is not just learning about your area or specific hunting grounds, but learning how you fit into nature. The woods will be there whether you choose to walk into them or not. Sit in the snow and listen. Breathe in the pure air that is cold and clean. Nature carries on whether you are there or sitting at home. One will begin to appreciate the majesty of the forest for all it holds, rather than the Pavlovian response by bugmen at a picture of any scene from nature without humans as precious. Men who have never stepped foot in a jungle or swamp will correct you for using those terms, and not the academic terms "rainforest" and "wetlands."

If you do hunt with regularity, you must learn how nature works. One must study the land and the beast. A hunter must understand the quirks and peculiarities of his prey. One will learn restraint and discipline because the prey's world is its own and you are a mere interloper. The hunt is not solely about the moment that an animal enters the hunter's line of sight. The hunt is about the entire process that culminated up to that moment. Each choice the hunter made brought him to that point. The hours of preparation and study now rest in his execution of what he knows. It is considered easy to one who has no comprehension of the duty a hunter has to himself and to the craft.

Like any craft and tradition, this too can be shared and passed down generations. From the dawn of man to our own age, the hunting party is a well-worn staple of masculinity. All hunting parties will have roles and rough hierarchy set into them. There is the man who organized the party, the experienced hunters who guide others, some who entertain and cook, and the new hunters that are not just gophers but the next generation to lead future trips. The hunting party creates inside jokes, stories that can only be known by those who attend, and fosters familial bonds. In our culture of chaos, a hunting trip allows for quiet moments that few get anywhere else with friends or family.

The thrill of accomplishment in bagging your first kill is heightened by the approval of your fellow hunters. It is a hurdle cleared to enter the club. The entire hunt is a process, and the failure to fell an animal is not a shame, but the man who calls hunting easy and barbaric actually fears failure. He fears shame. He fears not measuring up, and rather than acknowledge hunting as an accomplishment for someone else, it must be assigned no value. These voices of derision are focused merely on their specific status level and how it fits into societal programming. They fail to see the value in connecting with one's surroundings, pitting oneself against a living animal, and understanding nature.

CHAPTER 13

To engage in this world and make connections, one needs to be able to communicate. Sadly, our society does not look solely at actions, and is spellbound by any mortal that can speak well. Valuing the well-spoken man is fine, but too often, our society overvalues a man that has any rhetorical skills. Our weakness and apprehension with speaking makes us overvalue eloquence. This is a needed skill in a man that separates himself from the overfed, tired masses. A man who lives a life worthy of emulation will be misunderstood or considered eccentric if he cannot communicate effectively. The goal is to awaken an energy and stir a spirit in others. Converting men to push back on life and to sacrifice pleasures is much easier if one can explain the need to do so. A man who lives life with *thumos* becomes a contagious spirit if he can explain the joys of his journey.

Eloquence is a skill to work on, and it starts with simply overcoming apprehension and nervousness when speaking to a stranger. If you have been honing your skills and knowledge in different areas, you should be confident when speaking about them. The medium is the message, so the well-put-together man speaking eloquently about his passion or beliefs is a man that will entice others to follow him.

Charisma in this world is often just looking good and speaking well. Others merely project onto you what they want to believe to be true. Most people have superficial attachments and shallow thoughts, so the glib man can persuade many. One does not have to be a supreme salesman. No need to be a wizard with words. People clamor for a confident speaker that sounds the part. That your actions can deliver on words cements their allegiance. But even if you don't become a leader yourself, you may find a key supporting role as a great communicator.

Even before you speak, work on being a better listener and observer of cues in others. All messages must be tailored to the audience. In a group, there may be one listener who, if engaged, can turn the whole room towards your speech. Speak calmly, clearly and keep eye contact. Your voice is the voice of a leader confident in his capabilities and beliefs. Changes in tone should have a reason.

The man that looks away is a man whom people will question. How often does one hear, *"He couldn't even look me in the eye?"*

Listen to your voice. Not in your head, but record your voice and listen to how you speak. Do you sound confident and knowledgeable?

When you speak, relax your chest. A tight chest will affect your speaking voice. Relax your stomach. Relax your diaphragm. Smooth breathing will help you not just in how your voice sounds, but in how you pace a speech. You want to sound confident, calm, and ready for any question. You are the expert who will alleviate any concern and guide confused listeners.

Look in the mirror and practice how you deliver a speech or discuss a topic. Pay attention to the physical tics and quirks that you have that you were unaware you routinely do. Consider how you look when you stress a point, how you want to emote, and how your face should match each statement.

Start small. In a small circle at a party, can you control a conversation and get all to become engaged. Volunteer to present at work or in social clubs. If one's church has small programs, speak there. Even if the audience knows it is scripted and written in advance, they want to feel that you are extemporaneously talking to them.

Once you have ironed out flamboyant tics but still retain an individuality to your body movements, consider how you use your hands. To wave your hands around is to speak like a child or drunkard. Speakers that employ their hands too much seem overly excited and less serious. Consider deliberate movements and how you are using your hands. Do they complement your talking or do they distract?

Be careful to not raise your hands above your clavicle and wider than your shoulders. These are distracting movements and rarely match the content of a speech. Save raising your arms for declarations of victory and hallelujahs.

Be careful not to lock your hands into positions that convey stress or could be construed as defensive. No need to clasp your hands as in prayer, cover your crotch as if naked, or hold them behind your back as if a prisoner. Forget holding your arm as if wounded or hugging yourself as if in a straitjacket. You are not bored by your own speech!

Use your hands to accentuate your speech and to draw in others. Consider an imaginary box in front of you that is framed by your clavicle and waist and is as wide as the outer edge of your shoulders. Within this box, you can use your hands to emphasize a point by expressing the imagery you use or pointing to an individual to engage them.

Public speaking and presenting is a skill that can be worked, and has great value when forming any community. This is a skill that becomes a gift. If you have it as a gift, the ultimate sharing of it can be when you can speak for another at their funeral. The powers in oratory that you have developed can be the final praise you lay at a friend or family member's feet. In that moment, you can let a room of the most intimate friends know how special that person was not just to you, but to all of them. You will spread the memory of stories that mark that person's time on earth in your community.

We all have been taught, coached, preached to, and ordered by men. There is a difference between the typical man in an authority position and the inspirational leader. You can hear it in their delivery, see it in their face and body, and feel it when you recall their words. Many athletes have had the coach who uses his military stories as motivation. When some use them, they become just the latest fodder for digging deeper for a win. It might as well be plug and play for whatever topic the coach wanted at that moment to motivate his team. Then there are coaches that have carefully selected a specific story for the task at hand. Their delivery is different. There is a reason for telling you about a night on patrol in the jungle. For a few minutes, you hear about how to survive and win. That is the coach for whom you body check your opponent.

This is a transferable skill, and we see it all around us. The salesman who is a technical maven versus the salesman that makes you want to buy whatever he happens to be associated with. Customer relations experts who tell you all cares are addressed versus the public relations man who makes you feel you do not have a care in the world. The preacher that reads the book and implores you to live virtuously versus the preacher that helps you feel closer to God.

Some are born with this skill, but all must work at it. A skilled speaker will draw followers on whatever path he walks.

CHAPTER 14

As you develop your skills, you will collect friends. These bonds will deepen or break depending on how you cultivate them. No man can stand alone, no community is solid, and no civilization arises unless you have a *Männerbund*.

A *Männerbund* is a group of men that is organized and aligned with male instincts and drives. The size of the group does not matter. What matters is commitment to each other and shared goals. A *Männerbund* can dream up ideas, effectively execute plans, and create civilized space for order to form. Only from order can freedom grow.

From the playground, men form groups, and these groups start with the smallest and easiest of childish adventures. There are the silliest of jokes. This tendency continues through a man's life wherever he goes. The strength of his groups depends on the shared values and experiences between the men.

Developing friendships and a social circle is not something one researches. There is no Google search for how to form a band of men. It is hard to define, but is as old as time. There are shared in-jokes, there are small rituals, there are fun or dangerous adventures, and there are shared trials of fire. Nicknames developed by the group are a way to signal that not only is a man a member, but that he is *their* guy. That is *their* name for him, and you do not get to use it.

Two men do not simply say to one another that they are friends, and by swearing an oath, a group of five strangers does not become an organization ready to take on the world. No ritual has meaning if it is not after an accomplishment or rite of passage. No group of friends is really friends if they do not know the dreams and fears of their comrades. This process allows the friends to be able to insult or critique one another to make their friend a better man. There is an organic process, which cannot be bought, forced, or imposed.

Men are driven by innate desires to compete, and groups will refine and hone their skills against one another. In competition with looser groups, the skilled, cohesive group will win. Members of a strong *Männerbund* can anticipate one another's thoughts and actions. This makes them a superior hunting party, fighting force, or business partnership.

Small pioneer towns were often collections of men that believed in similar ideas, prayed to the same God, and brought their families along to build civilization on the plains or desert. They had to trust one another with their lives and their families' lives. These men had set roles to play, but could trust in one another to defend the territory and respect each other's rights and privileges. Just as not all men can be warriors, priests, or scholars, the *Männerbund* allows for specialization and a network of skilled and reliable men. A hierarchy will form and plans can be executed because order is found within the *Männerbund*.

A Marxist historian will tell you that the earliest Spanish settlers of Argentina were a rigid hierarchy that had class stratification and engaged in evil, inter-class oppression. The Marxist will write that this group viciously hunted outlaws. The historian will somehow lay all of the contemporary problems of Argentina on this initial outpost. Original sin in the form of one military camp.

Hidden in the analysis is the truth that the mission was barely over one hundred men. This was a *Männerbund* formed by the long sail across the ocean and the imposing challenge of settling an alien land. The men who signed up all shared the adventurous spirit, but had specialized skills and a variety of talents. A true leader, a captain, would determine who did what once the Promised Land was reached. Men held different jobs and had to answer up and down the chain of command because to do otherwise meant grave danger.

Those outlaws were men who betrayed the *Männerbund* and shirked their end of the contract between brothers. How else was such a dangerous expedition to enforce security an ocean away? There was safety and better survival as a group rather than devolving into an all against all fight in a new land. There is no understanding nor any context given, because the Marxist does not want you to consider that the brotherhood that founded the nation was virtuous, brave, and right.

The strength of a *Männerbund* depends on shared experience and struggle. Men relying on one another for a weekend of fun pale in comparison to men spending years together as a team, and even worse in comparison to men forming a community in hostile or new territory. The country club is one of the last vestiges of widespread male shared experiences. This is why it is attacked by the media and grievance groups.

A golfing crew is a tiny *Männerbund*. Men who golf together every weekend spend hours with one another to discuss everything. This is a smaller and weaker *Männerbund* than those facing war or existential threats, but it fosters more social cohesion than otherwise found among suburban neighbors.

Male groups develop strong feelings of cohesiveness, called *asabiyyah* in Arabic. There is group unity, cohesion, and a sense of a shared purpose. This communal feeling reminds the individual that while he may be striving for personal glory, he has responsibilities to his crew.

These *Männerbunds* were the war bands of ancient days that won ownership of physical space. They lived apart from settled cities and ate what they hunted, eschewing the farmer's life. The laws of nature educated them. They could draw no comfort from the community and gave no credibility to the community's mores and customs. Nature was their judge as well as teacher.

Shared experiences and trials reveal how each man relies on the other. Each man has a purpose and finds his place in the *Männerbund* and community beyond. This contradicts contemporary messaging about self-actualization and finding yourself. That message of individualism is also at odds with the group cohesive behaviors exhibited by the very media mandarins who push it. To complete the picture, individualism is pushed within a socialist framework teaching that no man does anything alone.

The contradiction makes sense when you consider how it is employed. They want you to think that you owe all fortune to their group and its arrangements. They do not want you to form your own cohesive group that could ever be independent of them. That group would be outside of their control.

This is why slowly but certainly they attack all private groups, all social organizations, and all clubs. They do not wish you to form your own hierarchy with values that would clash with theirs. They do not want leaders to arise that they have not educated and nurtured. They do not want homogeneous groups of men, because those groups have enough *asabiyyah* to be nearly unstoppable forces.

To slip the wildly different individual into a group will require a third party to bridge the gap. Who do you think can play neutral arbiter? Whose belief system will decide things then? The matriarchal, multicultural society around you relies on heavily armed men and the world's largest police and prison state just to cling to power. Even that system is a threat and they want to roboticize it, diversify it, and shackle it out of fear it will topple their civilian control.

These cultural gatekeepers also want you to think of yourself as an individual to compete all against all with every other man you meet. Their messaging is that there is no community. You are an individual seeking self-actualization. They want you atomized and neutralized. The beautiful garments of the hyper-individualized life are lined with lead.

Our environment has changed from a group game with a non-zero sum and shared outcomes to a zero-sum game where we think in smaller and smaller circles of, *"I win, he loses."*

This focus pushes men to become the richest man in a town of ashes. If you look at your hometown, you may recognize this. The owners of a meat processing plant that used third-world laborers did not care that the town became plagued by heroin. The *Männerbund* will force you to consider the needs of others in a pro-social way. Your ancestors raided villages together, burned them to the ground, and rode off with the women. This violence destroyed, but also created the civilizations that put you here.

The *Männerbund* respects its members' property, family, and women. The *Männerbund* is formed prior to the addition of women and children. It helps encourage family formation. What member of a *Männerbund* would seduce a friend's wife, harm a peer's child, or not care for his fellow member's family as if they were an extension of his? To be a part of a *Männerbund* is to fulfill these responsibilities and duties for your fellow members and to enjoy greater security for yourself. Acts that erode trust within the group are policed not just from external punishment, but through an internal awareness of the *Männerbund* as well as oneself.

The skills which you have developed combine with the skills of others to create a powerful corps of men to guide your community. These men can reassert a measure of dominance over physical space, from which order and civilization will again flow.

There is a moment in all of our lives where we first pass a threshold to manhood. In old cultures long gone, boys on the cusp of adulthood, maybe even pre-pubescent, would be sent out in the woods. It might have been to kill an animal. It might have been to merely survive. The ritual activity had begun, and when the boy would return, he would be an accepted member of the men of his tribe.

This progressed over time to when a boy would be asked to fight for his tribe. Youths were at Agincourt to help bowmen. This carried on down to modern times with the idealized image of the young drummer boy. Most nations used conscription, serving as a source of manpower but also as a state endorsement of the old ritual. There are American families where old family lore tells of how a young man had gone to Europe to fight in the Great War and come home to build a family. A generation later, that young man, now older and wiser, was sitting in his home explaining to his son that it was his turn, his time, and his duty to go off and fight the same fight again. The son returned home understanding his father, and the father respected his son. The ritual was renewed.

These rituals are nearly gone in our chaotic society and the chain of generations is broken for so many. The lowest replica for this now is the circle of friends that verbally haze a newcomer. If he sticks around, he is accepted, but if he leaves, well, he did not pass the threshold. There are moments, though, where we sense our elders letting us in as respected men. Maybe not men, but not as the boys we just were. It might have been the first time your father or uncle invited you hunting. It could have been the first time your father viewed you as a help when the car broke down and bragged about it to friends. You may have only held a flashlight and handed him the right socket, but you did it without complaint. It might even just be that invitation to sit by the fire and talk with the men.

Even just talk and sharing a fire matter. It is the oldest of human social settings. The written word is young in the history of humanity. All cultures had oral mythologies that if strong enough, both the myth and the people, made it to the printed word. The oral myth must contain the deepest of truths. It must explain in all ways the most important of lessons because remembering it is a precious tax on the mind. Even if it is your family and stories of how parents met or grandparents came to town, these stories are the special myths of your tribe.

The campfire chat acts in this manner as a ritual for acceptance and crossing the threshold into manhood. You can tell how you have grown with what is discussed. You grow and progress from being a young boy just listening, taking in the stories of those you may have known and those who passed on, to being a man that can engage with the storytellers. Eventually, you get old enough to be asked questions. You earn their respect. Your opinion matters. At the end, you tell the stories and determine when to invite new members to the fire.

It is entry to a circle that you respect. They now respect you. This happens in all male social groups. There are shared sacrifices and experiences. You accomplish things and earn invitation. The invitation matters. Legitimacy can never be imposed. It can be accepted and agreed upon by the group by your earned status. You seek the group, too. These are not merely people who exist in space. You have sought their company, their approval and their respect.

This drive which manifests itself as competition between men is the social dynamic of finding meaning and struggle. This is forged through hundreds of generations and so innate in those of us who survived the struggle that the system now resorts to sending its medical professionals to call traditional masculinity a problem. This traditional view carries with it traits and behaviors that supposedly damage men. These traits and behaviors also built civilizations and clawed out comfort in an indifferent universe.

At the heart of it, all men understand that they are born alone and without purpose. Men make their purpose. A woman is born and quickly learns that she is a cherished vessel for the next generation. Built in meaning and purpose is within her grasp. She can grow life, give birth to a living being who will love her. This is her power, and in our chaotic society, any man can help her make this happen. Her power to create is godlike.

Young men do not have this. Nothing is guaranteed. Men understand that the universe does not care. It is indifferent to man at best, malicious and bloodthirsty at worst. Because of the child, women will think the universe cares. It does not. A man does not have a guarantee that a child is even his. The universe can play tricks like that on him. Much of man's protective nature towards woman is this knowledge that the world is uncaring and a beautiful yet dark place. Every forest can inspire artists, yet within them lurk a myriad of dangers. This is why many of the horror stories of history involve a trip into the woods. It is the dark realm away from the safe fires within our homes.

Man has protected woman by placing her in the home by the children. Men approach the outside realm, bearing the burden of facing the unknown or dangerous world. Man tries to hide this from woman. It is hard to put into words this concern and the desire to protect them from seeing the indifferent universe for what it is. Yes, you may believe in an all-powerful God, but God's will is not often your will. Women have grown to resent this, yet the resentment is found in ignorance of the great void of indifference. Only now, female surgeons that realize their fertility window is closed and 40 more lonely years stare at them understand this horror. Only after losing that chance do they understand how protective the old arrangement was.

Women do not understand this poetry of struggle. This is why the moment in our lives when we stop wanting the respect and approval of our friends and start chasing the approval and comfort of women, we lose sight of meaning and purpose. It happens so young. It also is a modern creation: the sex-crazy teenager. The concept of girlfriends and boyfriends is barely 100 years old, yet we push this idea for younger and younger children.

The change is all-encompassing. A young man stops building his life and pulling people into it who value his intentions and goals. Women will always enter a man's social sphere. The stronger position to be in is the figure that women gravitate towards rather than a man chasing them.

Once young men switch in this drive, they reorient their entire worldview to pleasing the latest girl they want to date. This reorients their values and what they give status to towards a feminine perspective. They no longer seek the truth and walk that line, but seek to placate. If a man drifts further down this path, he grows to be one of those older men that looks at his wife for cues on how to react to anything, be it simple opinion questions or disciplining a child. The normal emotions and reactions a man has are no longer his. He has given up a portion of his mind and soul.

Because of the fight against the indifferent universe and the search for meaning, men understand the poetry of struggle. There is a deep intimacy with the cruelty of the universe. Overcoming the seemingly impossible to snatch any victory will pull a man's emotions out of him.

All modern men have that one tough friend. His father died, and he took it in stride. He did not shed a tear at his wedding or birth of his kids. He loses his job, and he searches for a new one. Broken bones, broken hearts, and broken cars do not faze him. One night, you will drink with him and his wife and she will almost angrily recall how she only saw him cry one time. Not cry, but tear up. You will hear her say, *"Of all times, we're watching Rocky and I look at him at the end and he's got tears in his eyes. Rocky!"*

She does not understand what your friend felt. Rocky was a bum, a palooka, and he was given one shot. He had a mousy-looking girlfriend and a washed up coach. He was scared. He just wanted to go the distance. At the end of the movie and fight, most viewers think Rocky won, but he did not. He lost, but he did not care. All that matters is he holds his woman and he did it. He fought the champion and did not back down. You sit there and chuckle at your friend's wife's story, but you know. You understand him in a way his wife will never understand.

It is the understanding that all men have. This is why physical contests and bloodsports appeal to men. Men understand the dedication that went into training for a season or just one night. They know that a fighter or athlete has punished their body, straining it to build strength and endurance. Diet, sleep, and lifestyle have all been altered to beat an opponent doing the very same.

No matter how one has trained, men understand that it all comes down to that one meeting. In a fight, it comes down to that first punch. This is the appeal of the underdog. The mismatched game still has to be played. The greater the mismatch, the less margin for error, which only adds to the poetry of the fight. No matter how a match-up appears on paper, it comes down to the man who rises to the event in that moment. The rise of mixed martial arts may confuse women, but to men it makes sense. Even if you trained for weeks or months, one punch might end it all. The universe does not care how fit you became or how hard you trained; one shot and you are done.

This is part of the romanticizing of lost causes. No matter the odds, you join for the fight, because in the fight, you find meaning. In conflict, you find brothers in arms. These men know the sacrifices and pain that you endured. They understand. Even if you come home emptyhanded and wounded, you were there. The Confederate veterans did not slink off to hide in obscurity, but went to reunions to remember.

There are successful men who spend thousands of dollars for a week-long camp to harden up. It is like a boot camp for middle-aged men. These are not the men's retreats of a generation ago, where men went to cry and get in touch with their feelings. There are no bongos slapped by the fire with crying time. These camps will hurl verbal abuse at them, run them through physical events, and talk to them in classrooms. The camps are facilitated by ex-special forces military veterans. This adds to the aura of danger and grit that the camp promises, because the marketing of special forces works on men seeking a camp to harden them up rather than look within.

The men are everyday men. Some might even be your neighbor, your boss, or your boss' boss. They have families and fortunes, enough to pay the high fees, but they feel empty. Something is missing. They have accumulated small accomplishments and checked off the boxes in life. Most likely, they have taken the safe course throughout their life to always do what was right. They were missing the struggle.

It is the struggle that defines you. Solzhenitsyn wrote of not wondering why good things happen to bad people or bad things to good people, but to concentrate on how events allow you to develop your soul. So many men have low opinions of themselves because they have never been pushed. They never faced the void and walked into the maw. No one wanted them hurt. Everyone told them to avoid pain, minimize suffering, and seek joy. They then grew to always avoid pain, no matter how temporary. They prioritized comfort.

The struggle allows you to find out about yourself in ways that drifting through an indifferent world simply chasing pleasure never will. Knowledge of this fight is what makes men the great risk-takers and disruptors of the world. Every adaptation, every improvement, and every innovation is from a man approaching a challenge in a way that no one else did and thinking that things could be better. It is a daunting task to change the world, appearing impossible when looked at from afar. It will never change if all seek pleasure and no pain.

CHAPTER 15

A *Männerbund* will understand the struggle you go through daily. This *Männerbund* is your circle of trustworthy men, but the broader brotherhood of men is a responsibility. If you can set a man on the path to understanding himself and how he fits into this world, then you have posted a wise sentry to hold firm against the feminizing forces of chaos. Beyond this defensive role, we need to remember that we are descended from risk-takers. Fraternities and clubs that engaged in duels would consider the scars from such duels as badges of honor. We must cultivate the masculine virtues of honor, aggression, and risk-taking. Men are not bound to the status quo. Men are disruptors that break static, dying orders. Men forge the new.

Women are drawn to men who take risks. Not simply in the cultural memes of men on motorcycles, but in the scientific proof of their attraction to men with facial scars. The scars signal risk-taking, proof that the man survived a challenge and maybe even left a foe for the worse.

Many men shy from risks because they feel abandoned and isolated. One strong friend emboldens the man. Consider the man at the bar that sees the woman making eyes at him. How many minutes does he waste standing there talking himself into it? Forget the need for a wingman; there is value in simply hearing one friend encourage him to walk across the room. Even if he fails, that friend is there for the man to circle back to, undoubtedly with the analysis that the female was not worth it anyway. Without his friend, does the man even walk across the room?

This is not simply a strategy for the established brother, but for potentials. Many men yearn for leadership and assistance, but pride prevents them from seeking help. This even afflicts men in obvious need for reform and guidance. There are many men that complain of minor pains and nuisances on their body. How often do grown men complain about their backs? Men in sedentary jobs complain about this! They avoid training heavy for their back. They fear a deadlift or a row will send their back into serious pain. Then they do a set of deadlifts, shrug heavy weights, or row with ferocity. They wait for the pain to come. The next day, those muscles are not in pain. They are tired from the workout, but the complaints of old wither away the more they train. Their back was not in pain due to injury. It was just weak. It had not been challenged.

This is the case with many issues. Men conjure up weaknesses and maladies that are not real, but are only symptoms of inactivity and a life of no challenges. Many men claim there are no mountains to climb. They are wrong. The mountains are there. No one is challenging them to conquer them. They will not climb the nearby hill because they will not take the first step. They will think about it, talk about it, and rationalize why they will not or should not do it. They do this with an entertainment complex around them encouraging them not to take risks. They sit in isolation, physically and metaphorically, alone with thoughts seeded by outside voices telling them to take the safe path and avoid the challenge.

It takes one voice to shake them of this. One voice that sets an example of having taken that first step. It takes the voice of someone who has sought challenges and would seek the challenge with them.

CHAPTER 16

There is a word, short and simple, that you must reacquaint yourself with for this walk: "no."

This decayed culture asks men to bend and be flexible in every single realm. There is no belief that they won't ask you to compromise to accommodate some new grievance group. Too many men tolerate the intolerable simply because they do not want to say no. Their mouths can form this word, but they don't say it because they are afraid that the reaction of others would require them to lead.

You descended from men that settled wild lands and carried off women for brides, moving through the dark forest to your tribe's camp. Act like it. Try a confident and strong *"no,"* followed up without apology and by going back to what you were doing.

How many marriages are turned into slave-master relationships because a man could not simply say no and laugh at the ensuing outrage? She will get angry and she will move on. Those husbands suffer through miserable lifetimes because they did not want to deal with a painful argument. Think of the women that threaten or outright withhold sex from their husbands due to small disagreements. It is not the act, but even the threat shows the man's weakness. He has shown that he is weak there and will cave for the tiniest morsel of physical gratification, because if a woman thinks the threat will work, sex has completely devolved to a scheduled activity for her. The passion and animal spirits are gone. She knows he cannot say no and deal with her upset at him. She knows he will not verbally retaliate with barbs that cut far deeper than simply withholding sex.

How many children are spoiled and grow to be incapable adults because a father could not say no? The child given everything melts down in adulthood when they meet the grinder of reality. Strategic nos would have saved them future pain. If a child melts down, remove the child from the room. The child may say, *"I don't love you anymore."* Answer, *"Good for you."* Be sure to remind them of that statement the next hour or day when they do declare their love for you.

Too many seek the path of least resistance for right now with no regard for the dangers it creates in their future. A friend does not break up with his girlfriend because of the potential drama. He fears her lashing out at him. A few years later, he gets engaged because they've been together long enough. He could not say no. Eventually, the small defeats and retreats back him into a corner. He gets divorced and says the worst of things, *"I never really loved you,"* to his ex-wife during the proceedings. The drama and pain of the divorce dwarfs what he would have faced at age 21. If a child is involved, more lives are damaged. All because he could not say no. It is easy to go along and easy to not fight. It is also easy to lay down in front of a steamroller and be squashed. It is men acting weak and not wanting to assert themselves.

No is not purely a negative. No is considered a bad thing in our permissive society. The no for you can be a savior. Glory-hound coworkers ask for your help and you know they won't credit you? No, that is your project. Friend is getting a vasectomy before he even marries? No, I will not validate your odd choices. Single mom declares on social media she does a father's work? No, you aren't even a good mom. This man feels like a woman sometimes but other times feels like a man so they have a continuously changing set of names? No, and maybe get some help.

Look around you at the groups that thrive and grow even in this age of chaos. There is a common trait to them. They police their borders and behavior of members. There is a cost to defecting and bucking the norms and mores. They say no to bad behavior. They shame behavior detrimental to the group's stability and continuity because they know that the group provides identity and a sense of purpose and belonging.

If someone defies the virtuous norms, they lose the security and benefits of being part of the group. Today, people are rewarded by the ruling class' status system for defecting from their *thede* and being open to anything different. They have not had it instilled in them to show allegiance to their home group over the ruling class' desired pool of humanity. Those who defect from their innate groups do not hear no. These defectors do not see the value in strong bonds with their immediate tribe versus the tenuous, transactional connection they have to the ruling class. These defectors have had their immediate social circles attacked and often destroyed by the ruling class.

Men are afraid to say no not just because of the recipient's reaction, but are afraid of what others might think. Such men have fallen into the trap of social status obsession where the omnipresent Borg is watching. This is a Borg that allows degeneracy to flourish, but such men value their opinion. For a moment, they will disapprove. He fails to see that they rarely if ever think about him.

A life spent submitting, shrinking, and bowing to others will make one invisible. At the minimum, one becomes a man of no consequence. No civilization was founded and built by emasculated men. No is a powerful word. It is also one where if you hold firm, the target and witnesses will see this and respect you for taking a stand. Even with the smallest of things, no improves your ability to weather storms and preserve truth and tradition from the whirlwind of modernity.

CHAPTER 17

As we age, there will come many opportunities to allow others the moment to shine or to unburden us. These opportunities come often in old age, but even when younger, there are moments where we need help. Many of us are afraid to say *"I can't"* with regards to a task we normally can do. Even when afflicted with disease or recovering from an injury, many men still want to do what they normally have the capacity to do. We want to feel useful. It is wiser to recognize when those moments hit us and when others want to help. It is safe and good to seek help.

It is not just to alleviate our loads, mental and physical, but to offer other men the opportunity to help. In these instances, a son has the opportunity to prove growing skills and strength. A friend or coworker can prove their personal skills are handy. They show value in a world where we are never quite sure where we stand. To deny these opportunities is to prevent the full expression of your fellow man. They do not reduce your standing as an individual or as a part of the family or community.

There is the clichéd image of the old man who still wants to shovel snow during and after a snowstorm and reluctantly allows his grandson to do the job in his stead. 20 years earlier, it was the little boy watching the grown man throw snow over banks, but now it is the old man watching the youngster toss the snow away. Sometimes this is done through the same window with only their positions reversed. This is the younger man's opportunity to prove worth and show he can do it. There is the recognition that you have done this for me, so I shall do this for you. It is part of belonging to a family, a circle of friends, and a community. One has to allow for others to share in the work, the joy, and the struggle.

There is not just a physical component to this, but the mental, emotional, and spiritual. In admissions of failing or showing humility, we welcome the sharing of others. These open up opportunities for others to share with us things they may normally not mention. Individuals who have been to substance abuse recovery meetings often make friendships that last for decades. Alcoholics Anonymous started with two men just talking together. We allow someone to help us and console us, showing us we are not alone with their stories. Therefore, we provide them with a power they may never have known they had.

In the ritual of death, these opportunities to share are ever-present. This allows younger people, people you may have raised or guided, to show that they do belong and that they have a role. This is part of delegating tasks and allowing you to focus on grieving or consoling someone else who seems inconsolable. Death is an emotional time where we not only remember the person who has perished, but evaluate our lives. Roles within a family change with each death. The rituals and small tasks at this time help people process what they must do now within the family.

Spiritually, when we deny admitting the need for help, we deny the others the opportunities for earning that blessing from God for helping us in a time of need. This is an important moment. We live in a world where people wonder about meaning and how they fit into the bigger picture. When these moments come, it gives people an opportunity to provide relief and aide someone. Service to another, especially a loved one, is part of the grand vision of God's love. People find meaning and love in this service. It is an act of love and care. People will find satisfaction with their place within the grand ensemble. They will receive God's blessing for such sacrifice and work.

This plays into admitting our faults, errors, or sins to another. Showing forgiveness and good judgment to allow someone who has wronged us a seat at the table is a sign of strength and wonderful act. There is power in condemning others and casting them out, whether from a community or merely a group of friends. There is just as great a force of power to forgive another. To allow them to return to the tribe. This is not the cheap, contemporary forgiveness that people spout on television when a reporter asks them if they forgive the killer of their family. This is man to man. Sin and forgiveness is between man and his God, but it is also between a man and an authority in his community. Yes, God shall judge man in the afterlife, but here, right here on Earth, we are judged by our fellow men.

When we ask forgiveness, we are allowing another this role. They have this power now. They can make this judgment. This is not just anybody, as we select who we ask forgiveness from and who we value enough to approach. Victims of abuse may see their abuser die and despite the wrongs done, the victim will still say after a funeral, *"That bastard could never admit what he'd done."* There is no erasing what happened, but that victim wanted to go through the ritual. Even a deathbed request for forgiveness would allow the big moment. The moment where they could be judge, be powerful, and make that decision. When denied it, the victim will often say that they would have told the person off. We know this is a lie. They wanted to hear the request because they wanted to forgive. It is the chance, like any troubled relationship, for the two to come together for a joyful resolution and reconciliation. We know what a blessing it is to relieve another.

These are not moments of weakness. There is no shame in showing this vulnerability. This is when we admit that situations are beyond our control. We do need assistance just as we have assisted others throughout life. A lifetime of guiding and helping others should provide one with perfectly capable friends and family to aide one during a moment of crisis.

***

One of the disabled processes in our culture is our unstoppable, biological aging mechanism. Physically and now mentally, people have stopped the natural process of aging. Modern man not only fights the idea of growing old and frail, but now actively fights growing up. This is a deep fear of death, as man, having lost touch with the idea of an afterlife and an immortal soul existing in another plane, clings to existence and believes not growing up means he can deny death. This reveals the fraudulence of the "spiritual but not religious" crowd as there is nothing spiritual to them. They have lost touch with what old believers would have considered a soul. They think of it as consciousness as they have an empty approach to the soulful, hence their obsession with describing things as *what it means to be human.*

Aging emotionally is a process of accumulating experiences, good and bad, and growing from the struggle that one engages in as well as the good fortune. Aging involves assuming new roles as one changes from boy to man, bachelor to husband, nephew to uncle, fighter to worker, son to father, and father to grandfather. These experiences build and are stored away in your soul's compendium. It is the human experience and marks time.

We see this not just with individuals, but with generations. Some say life is akin to a day. We are born, the sun rises; we live, the sun is high in the sky; we die, the sun sets. This is not a good fit for what it means to truly live. A man's life is like a storm. Clouds gather and the wind changes. No one quite knows what to expect. The storm builds. People believe they can predict the storm and its features.

Once the pieces are in place, the clouds full of rain, the winds at full speed, and the skies darkened, then we see the storm's full might. Storms rarely go as predicted. All storms are different. Some pour down for hours, and some pass within an hour. Some are full of thunder and lightning, leaving people shook. Some are just thunder that never quite comes. Some just pass through and let you play in their presence.

A man's blood may run hot, or he may have ice in his veins, and this applies here as well. A summer thunderstorm warns you about its power. What of those cold, quiet men? Like the snowstorm where everything goes still and cold but one can feel that it is going to snow, these men give no hint at their potential. Some of the coldest, most ferocious storms drop snow, leaving you guessing and hoping that it passes soon. A storm breaks, lessens, and grows weaker as it ages. It is gone. All storms pass, and so do men's lives. How it raged may create a memory, and if faint in force, it will be quickly forgotten.

Even the approach to assuming roles has gone through a metamorphosis that inverts or subverts each role. A parent wants to be a friend. This does not just destroy the parent-child hierarchy, but keeps the individual from growing up into the parent role. They want the privilege of saying they are a parent, but not the duties. Deep inside, they did not want to become the square and out-of-touch parent that they viewed their parents as being. People over 40 cannot handle being considered out of touch or square, but it happens to everyone as culture changes. To admit they are the parent with all the authority that comes with that is to admit they are older.

Some would say we have a youth culture. We celebrate youth. Not quite. Currently, we celebrate the features associated with the young. We have no use for the old. It is said that before the Great War, young men grew beards and wore glasses to appear older. To be older was to be wiser and experienced. After the conflagration of that war, the culture changed orientation. All of that aged wisdom was discredited in that war. There was still the sense that youth culture was just that; for the young. It never stops now no matter how macabre the efforts. Our elderly take pills to recreate the sex lives they had decades earlier. The middle-aged inject themselves with biological weapons to erase the proof of their age. Everything is done to freeze people in time at an eternal 30.

The freezing idea is not just a physical phenomenon. This is not just 50-year-old women with Botoxed, wrinkle-free faces and augmented breasts to appear 30. The resistance to growing older can be found in adults who become consumers of children's toys and obsessed with media products originally intended for children. They may laugh at a cartoon that your child also watches. This is not passing laughter at a slapstick antic on a random screen. These frozen individuals seek out this entertainment. Mentally and emotionally, they do not want to grow old. They do not want to engage with the adult world or enjoy the history of cultural products from centuries of efforts. The worst offenders are the slovenly-dressed adults that will deconstruct and analyze cartoons yet refuse to engage in a text more adult that Harry Potter. They will repeat the page length of the Harry Potter books as if this gives the writing weight, covering up that the series is written, designed, and paced for children.

If they never consider themselves old, they do not get old. To grow old is to grow closer to death. They are scared of death. This ties back to our obsession with the presentation of youth. Some of this is due to our sequestering of the elderly into nursing homes. The thought of growing old becomes a thought of being in a nursing home, which then translates into waiting to die. Our society's damning of the elderly to slow death centers is one of its greatest crimes. This also stems from our society's obsession with spending as much time, money, and effort on scraping an extra year or two of life.

Can you spot someone who is going to cling and claw at every single day? They will not live with a zest to the additional years, but they will be the type to take whatever pill and endure whatever procedure for an additional year. Listen carefully the next time someone dies. Listen to their reactions or commentary. Hear them chastise someone who goes off dialysis and just quit at 75. Listen for them to question or even mock someone's decision to go off their meds in their seventies or God forbid, sixties and die a year later. Look at them and know that they will be the man or woman popping ten pills and helping pharmaceutical companies hit their quarterly earnings. Not to live, but to keep death at bay.

This is where realizing death comes for us all and at any time is nature. Many cannot face it themselves and cannot handle losing those they love. When our loved ones die, we feel pain and all go through this. Mourning is the most natural of acts because it affects us all. It is also a natural moment to take stock in one's life. It makes us touch our mortality. The gravestone often has the last name that we have. The parent or grandparent often is the person we resemble the most.

What have they done? What have you done? How will you chose to honor them? Will people honor you? It is good to sing their praises, but hagiographies are children's tales. There is most likely something in every person you know who passes on in your lifetime that you share in common with them. Learn from their mistakes. Consider the errors they made. Think of their strengths and emulate them. To emulate and copy them is to honor their existence. This destroys the nihilists who argue how nothing is meaningful and everything is impermanent and useless.

We say goodbye in this world on a marked day. The hysterics or tears of that day are not the end. You carry them with you as a memory to share. You can reduce everyone you know down to a 30-second commercial. You could spend the rest of your life telling your kids and others the 30-second commercial of their life. That would be cheating them. It would be disrespectful of all that they were. A human life should not be reduced to a catchphrase, one anecdote, and a physical description. To care about them should force you to curate your memories about lost loved ones. Our society is a disposable society, but we can fight this by celebrating those who have gone.

***

Children are gone or children never showed up. Woman or no woman in your life, you still are part of your community. You can still lead. There are always brothers of the tribe that could use your help, your counsel, and your accrued wisdom. No man leads an army of one. Your gifts and skills are used to help others. A lifetime of wise counsel breeds a reputation. Do not believe those that say reputation does not matter any longer. People say this to conform to the broadcasts of the cultural mandarins. As social trust decays, reputation will matter more. Once a reputation is developed for wisdom and *phronesis,* a wider network of individuals will seek you. The role will be akin to a grey king or guru on the mountaintop. Even if alone, others seek such a man.

Some spend their youth looking for such a man, and many enter the adult world confused and without a guide. Voices hammer at them to chase the ephemeral and new. This constant rotation of consumable experiences will bring titillation, but will sow confusion and unfulfillment. The swirl of society will leave them forever moving, not grounded. What could they possibly latch onto when their traditions have been rooted out? It is not firm earth they travel on, but the sea.

They will look for you. Their entire social network has been stripped and slashed, forcing them to seek some substitute for the old figures of authority. They subconsciously do this even if they vocally deny it. You have built the foundation and lit the beacon for these ships. They do not know they are looking for you until the storm hits, but you then guide them. You have been carefully constructed and tended to meet that need. You show them the way.

You are the light in the darkness. In lighter times, they smile and respect your existence. They thank you for standing strong. They know they can rely on you. They know they need you. They may never publicly admit it yet they know.

The crime in this chaos is to admit that a man is needed. Society laughs at the need for fathers, husbands, and male teachers, and it promotes the matriarchal society. You know the deep truth. They do not just need it, but they deeply crave captains. They deny it, then cry at the funerals of old men. They know what they have lost when the grey-bearded patriarch is finally gone. The years they spent denying the value of his stories, skills, and experience are matched by the years after his death that they lament his passing. To cry at the passing of a father, brother, teacher, and friend is no shame. A man knows the burden his fellow men must carry. No woman knows.

Laugh at the woman who says she does both jobs, father and mother. Do not begin by refuting her. Do not nod your head and validate her claim. Do not let others support this. Laugh. Laugh hard and tell her why. She may be the only parent. She may do the work of two, but she will never be a father.

These single mothers complain about the men they date. The men are moody, flaky, emotional, and not like the "real men" these women recall from some yesteryear. These women do not see that these men they date are from the first wave of the ocean of men raised by women. These men are copying their mothers because they had no father. If this same single mom claims to play the father's role, then like her peers, she is a failure.

These women do not stop to ponder the consequences of their claims to be playing with the boys. They do not consider the full male experience, but cosplay the particular parts the system wants them to play. She works hard for the corporation. She has meaningless sex. She acts tough. She isn't afraid to fight. She then wonders why women are depressed more, committing suicide more often, and why one in four are on mental medication.

Playing at just a few parts of the male role drives women to medication, drinking, and despair. It is woman's ignorance of masculinity that they would ever dare to claim she was performing a father's role. No man would claim to do a mother's role, for he knows he could never be a mother. A dog may jump around and act like a cat, but it is still a dog.

You plant seeds for a later blossom. You set stone to withstand the storms of tomorrow. You grapple with the soul for the eternal. You say no and mean it, and derisive disappears in a moment.

CHAPTER 18

It is tempting to read this and see a checklist. This book is not a checklist, but a guide. The worst thing to do is to consider this guide as a to-do list. One does not carve a personality or a life out of finding new passions and unlocking your abilities. Those abilities and passion must be tested, they must face obstacles, and they must be stoked or refined. One does not consider this a to-do list to be a man's man once enough power-ups are collected. One would be a hollow man.

We all have seen this hollow man. This is not what people call the empty suit. The empty suit is shallow, a lightweight, or a nonentity. Not much is expected of the empty suit because he is just another guy. The individual man is irrelevant. The hollow man still has the form of man. The empty suit by definition is a suit without a man in it, signifying just how nonexistent the individual in question is. The hollow man has developed many of the skills mentioned in this book, possibly all. There is a problem. That energy that states "no" and has the power to hold it is absent. It is not a moment of hesitation or a single breakdown. It weaves its way through his life. The moment to force his will at work becomes saved for a better time. The time to tell his wife things need to change is kicked down the road. He is afraid to take the risk.

We have all seen this man. He may be a relative or close friend. He comes to us for help, and we give counsel. The final moment is in his hands. It is his responsibility to act. There is only so much you can do for him, because even with a solid social network, all men are alone. These hard acts are what round out the duties and character of a man. In this regard, there is emptiness to the hollow man's existence.

This is not to say that he avoids study, gym, or church. With his appearance and manners, one would not expect it. This is not to say he avoids discussion of exerting one's will. He may even relish discussing it. He just cannot follow through and act. He cannot pull the trigger. All cultures have some word or phrase for this, and if they do not, they can identify it at the first faltering. A man who follows through and exerts his will makes those around him react strongly to a momentary lapse in behavior. The hollow man's misstep is met with derision or an eye roll from those who witness it. It is expected, anticipated, and sometimes even encouraged by those wishing to humiliate him.

These hollow men are not just around us in everyday life but on the global stage. The last shah of Iran, Mohammad Reza Pahlavi, may be the best example. The Shah was raised in luxury and educated to reign in Iran. He knew what his father had done to pacify the land. He had heard the stories and seen the results of his father's work subduing the different power centers of the nation and forging a daring modernization program. The last Shah spent a lifetime filling out the role with the pomp and circumstance of being a monarch. He had his playboy streak, he carried himself as a monarch, and was a fantastic interview subject. He spoke of the mystical nature of his role and his connection to the people he ruled.

It was a well-rehearsed and polished act. Those who met him in private marveled at how the Shah could be informal, relaxed, and look normal, but the moment he knew he would have to face a crowd, the transformation in his body and mind would begin. The loose and relaxed man would be willed into the steel-spined Shah. The Shah was similar to a television character. Mohammad Reza Pahlavi was the real man. No matter how hard he tried, the man was who he was and the Shah but a role.

Whether in his inner circle or a diplomat stationed in Iran, it was known that in times of crisis that the Shah held on because someone else ordered the shootings, the crackdowns, and the difficult task of exerting his will on rebels. He would freeze in crisis moments with internationally known embarrassments. The Shah knew everything about his role except for those difficult lessons his father taught via example with pacifying the countryside. He admitted to his closest advisors about not wanting to be a butcher to maintain his hold on the nation of Iran. As the Shah aged, there were moments where diplomats would openly question if he had grown and hardened. The implication being that to be a true ruler is to have that hard edge to go along with the pageantry.

Mohammad Reza Pahlavi had forgotten that a monarch must perform all of the duties of a sovereign. No kingdom was ever won without bloodshed. At some point, a leader has always won a crown by clearing out rivals, declaring himself owner of that space. His legitimacy is proven by his command of men who will perform violence. While a lower-stakes situation, this is the same as the hollow men in our lives. It might start with a simple no, but the inability to deny another will guarantee the inability to perform all duties that earn one the right to command, to secure loyalty, and enjoy authority.

Failing to fulfill all of those duties, one reveals that the refinement of one's soul or masculinity is nothing but a mere hobby. It is a surrogate activity to pass the time.

***

Perhaps you read this and laughed. Perhaps you rolled your eyes. You are intoxicated on their messaging. You have submitted to their standards. Rise up.

What would they call such a man that strove to fulfill these instructions? Look at what they call your brothers.

The man who works out? He is an overcompensating narcissist.

A grey-haired man in a sports car? He's a nervous man with a mid-life crisis.

An unmarried man at 35? He is a boy afraid of commitment.

A man who doesn't date single moms? He's a guy who won't man up.

A man committed and dedicated to his work putting in long hours? A workaholic.

A man who plays video games after college? A man-child, a Peter Pan.

If he dates younger women? An immature creep.

Enjoys a drink during the week? A drunk.

A man who gives a woman unwanted attention? Creep. If he does so at work? He's now unemployed.

Won't pay for a date? He is a broke cheapskate.

A father present when his daughter has a sleepover? He's a potential molester.

Prefers thin, feminine women? He's brainwashed.

A man has a deep, meaningful friendship with a fellow man? He is a closet case.

If he wants his wife to stay home and raise their children? He's an oppressive patriarch.

If a man values chastity? He is a slut-shaming oppressor.

If a man likes the look of 18-year-old women? He's a borderline pedophile.

If a man treats a woman like a lady? He is the pal a woman never dates.

A man who doesn't keep up with the latest fads? He is an out-of-touch goof.

If a man fights for custody of his kids? He is a second-class citizen.

If a man wants to remove his genitals and wear a wig, he is courageous and beautiful.

These are the labels created by a sick society that has lost touch with the essence of man. These are the labels of the deviant side of the spiritual war that smears any attempt to embrace the masculine traits that create order and civilization. This society glorifies vice and eschews virtue. What legitimacy do the labels of an inverted society have?

Every single male virtue is treated as a vice for which we must repent and apologize. Simply exhibiting these traits makes one a suspect in the eyes of the bugmen. They do not even refute arguments or debate, but rather spit out labels. These insects are afraid of testing their fullest potential as men. Unaware of the substitution, they focus on the latest technology and dream of transhumanism. They would rather turn their body into a machine than to optimize body and mind through training and challenge. Destroy their humanity rather than fulfill it. Cybernetics receives applause, but the bicep curl is an expression of toxic masculinity.

This inverted society has tried to remake man to further its destructive designs. Man and woman, family, marriage, and fatherhood predate all societies. Their destruction is the destruction of civilization.

When you say no and are called some label, remember the label is powerless unless you respect the reaction of the one applying the label. Your actions have caused a reaction in them. They are always defining any discomfort or challenge to their beliefs down to a demonic sin.

We, the labeled men, provide the catalyst for others who are still drugged and inert. They root for us, and courage begins to stir in them.

Still others cannot act. This era is defined by the sedentary. They sit. They consume. They are not even passive travelers, but blinkered mules. They select between the narrow but new and exciting options laid before them. This applies not just to the oligopoly offering consumer products, but to their core being. They assume labels prefabricated for them by distant marketers. They assume and discard them like tissues. This is a disposable society, and expressions of their essence will also go into the trash heap. They junk an identity, yet expect to be remembered. They forget their ancestors and family folklore, but expect others to honor them.

Your pursuit of traditional ideals frightens them. Modern man fears not the unknown, but the known that he fails to honor, the known against which he fears he cannot measure. Some recognize the sickness around them but fail to act. Your acts are rebellions against this sick society. It is in contrast to the stasis, ossification, and decay of others. They will attack you.

Your pursuits are for you, your line, and your community, not them. They openly reject and mock that which you value. They shout into the void using any medium to be heard, "I exist." You act and build to be remembered through the ages.

Your family may have a painting of a long gone ancestor. Your town may have a statue of a solitary man, a soldier, or a pioneer. Look at those men. They do not look directly at you. Their eyes are on the unseen future. They watch the land they left. They do not look at you when you stand right before them. They look at what you have done.

ABOUT THE AUTHOR

Ryan Landry is a middle American family man. He lives with his wife and children in a small town.

terrorhousepress.com

Made in the USA
Middletown, DE
23 May 2021

40276213R00076